I0472257

Morgan State University - School of Architecture and Planning - BSAED

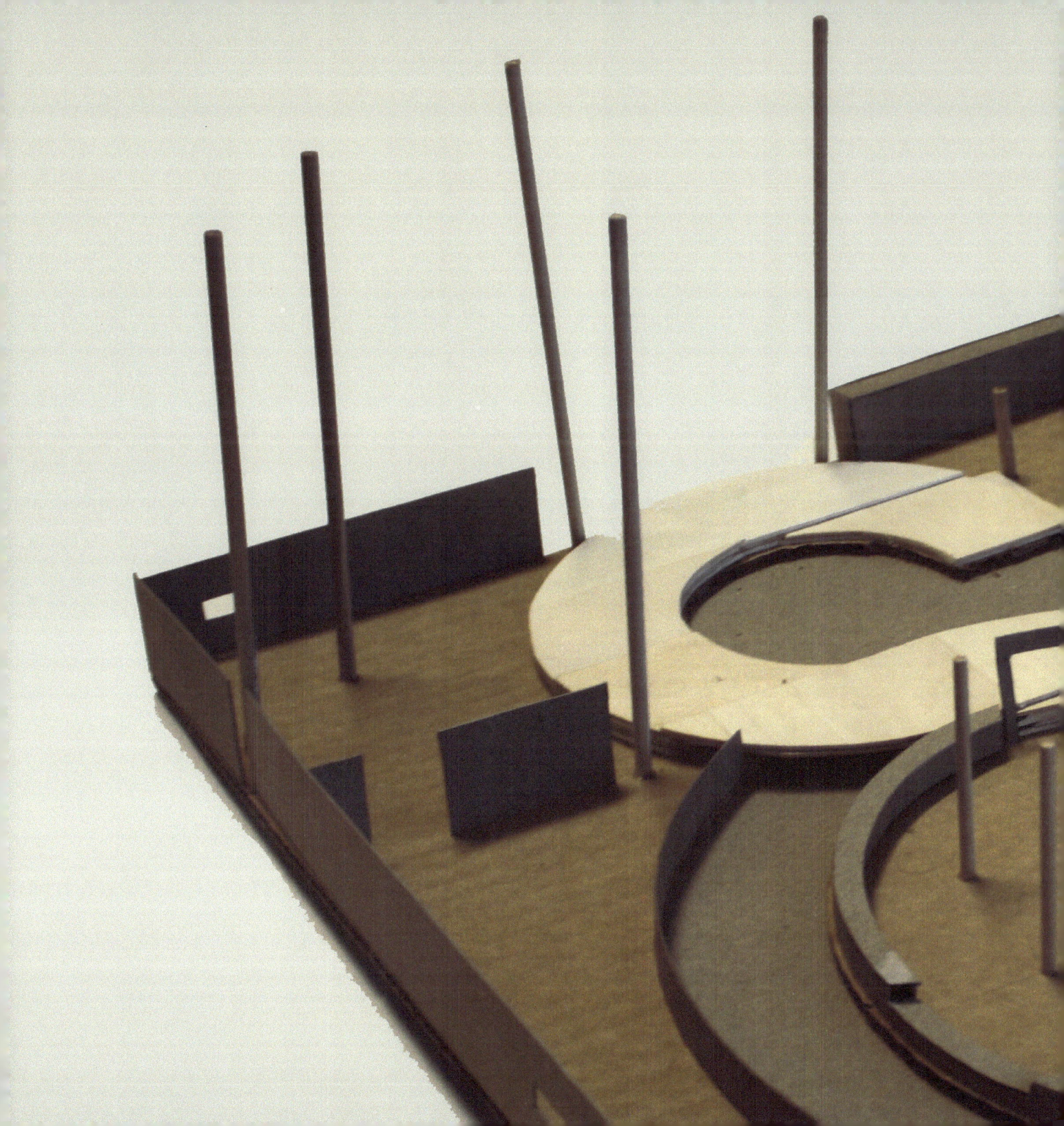

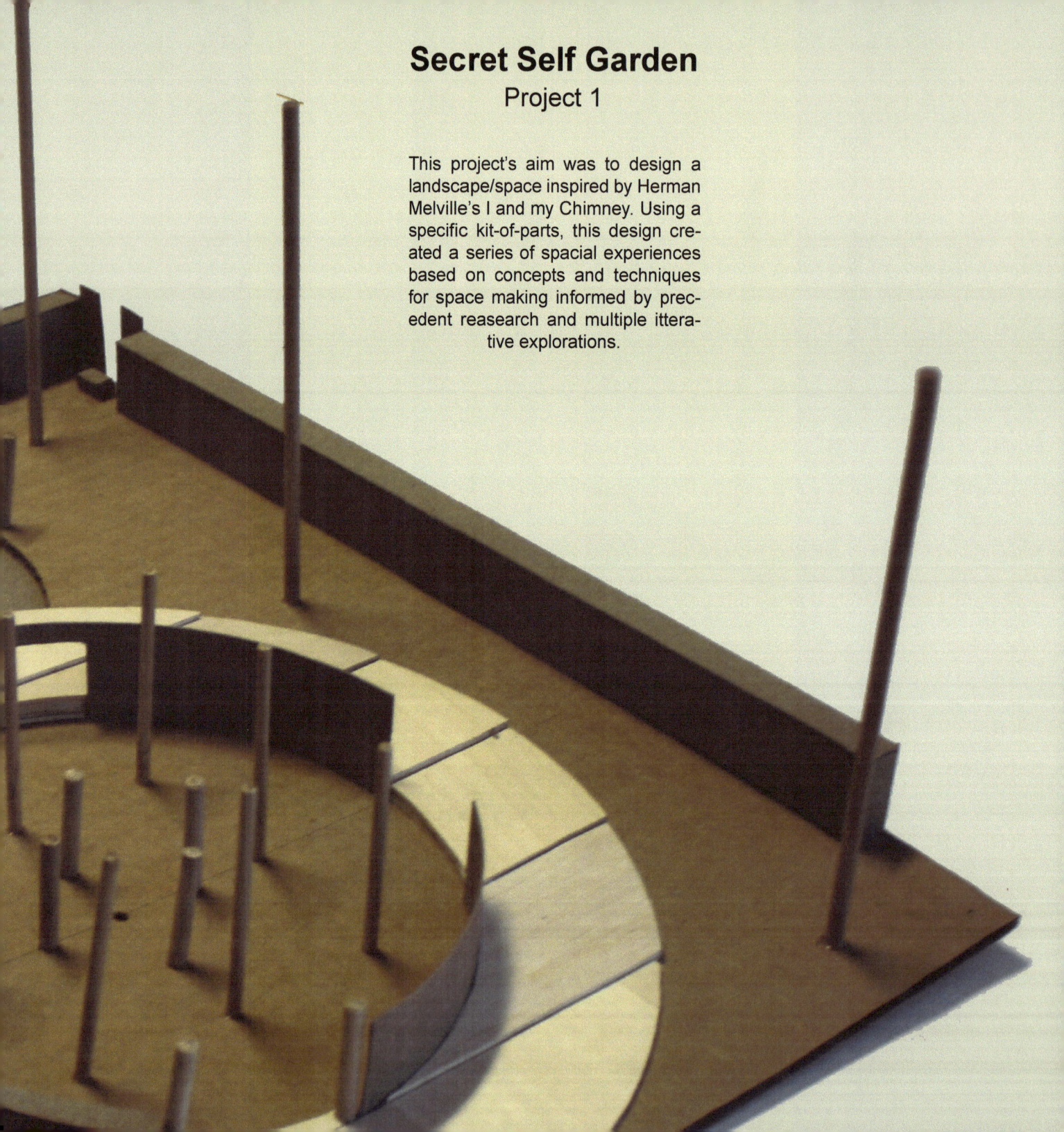

Secret Self Garden
Project 1

This project's aim was to design a landscape/space inspired by Herman Melville's I and my Chimney. Using a specific kit-of-parts, this design created a series of spacial experiences based on concepts and techniques for space making informed by precedent reasearch and multiple itterative explorations.

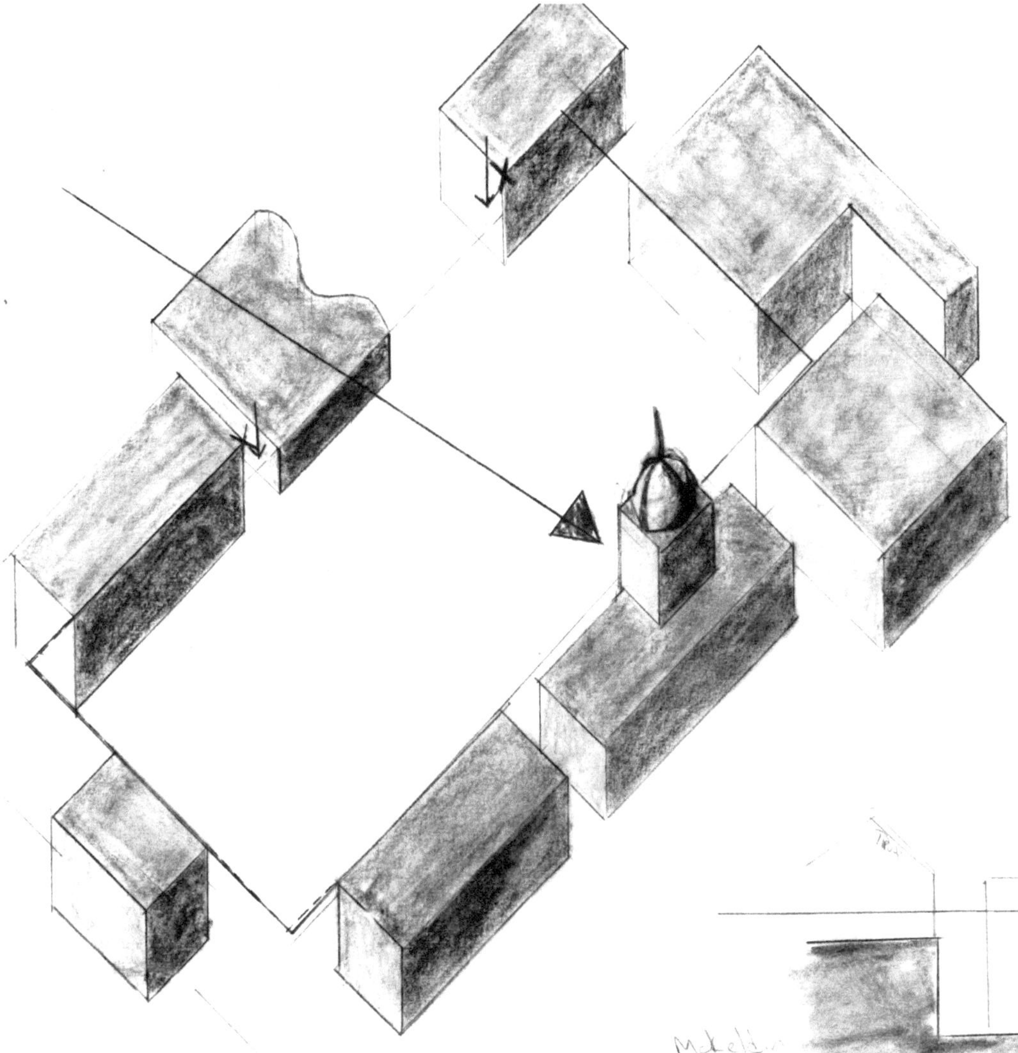

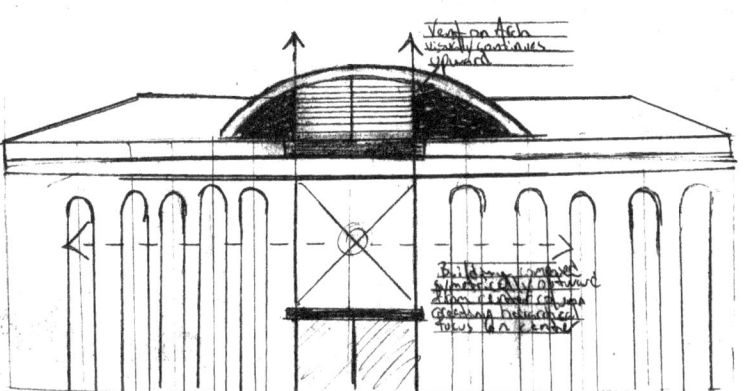

The first stages of this project heavily focused on developing diagramatic commnication and drawing skills.

Our initial precedent analysis was of the campus quad at Morgan State University where we studied and examined patterns of order with its design.

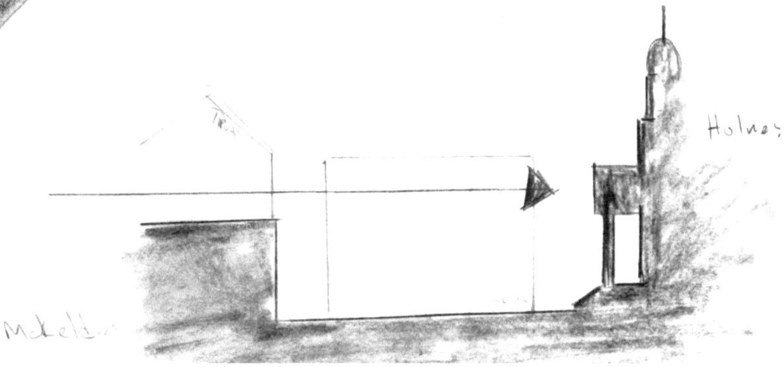

The next phase of precedent analysis was of sites that we could not physically visit or observe. To the right are diagrams of Miller House and Gaden by Eerio Saarinen and Parc de la Villette by Bernard Tschumi. These two shared elements of a common ordering principle of a regulating grid. This grid concept went on to inform my resulting design.

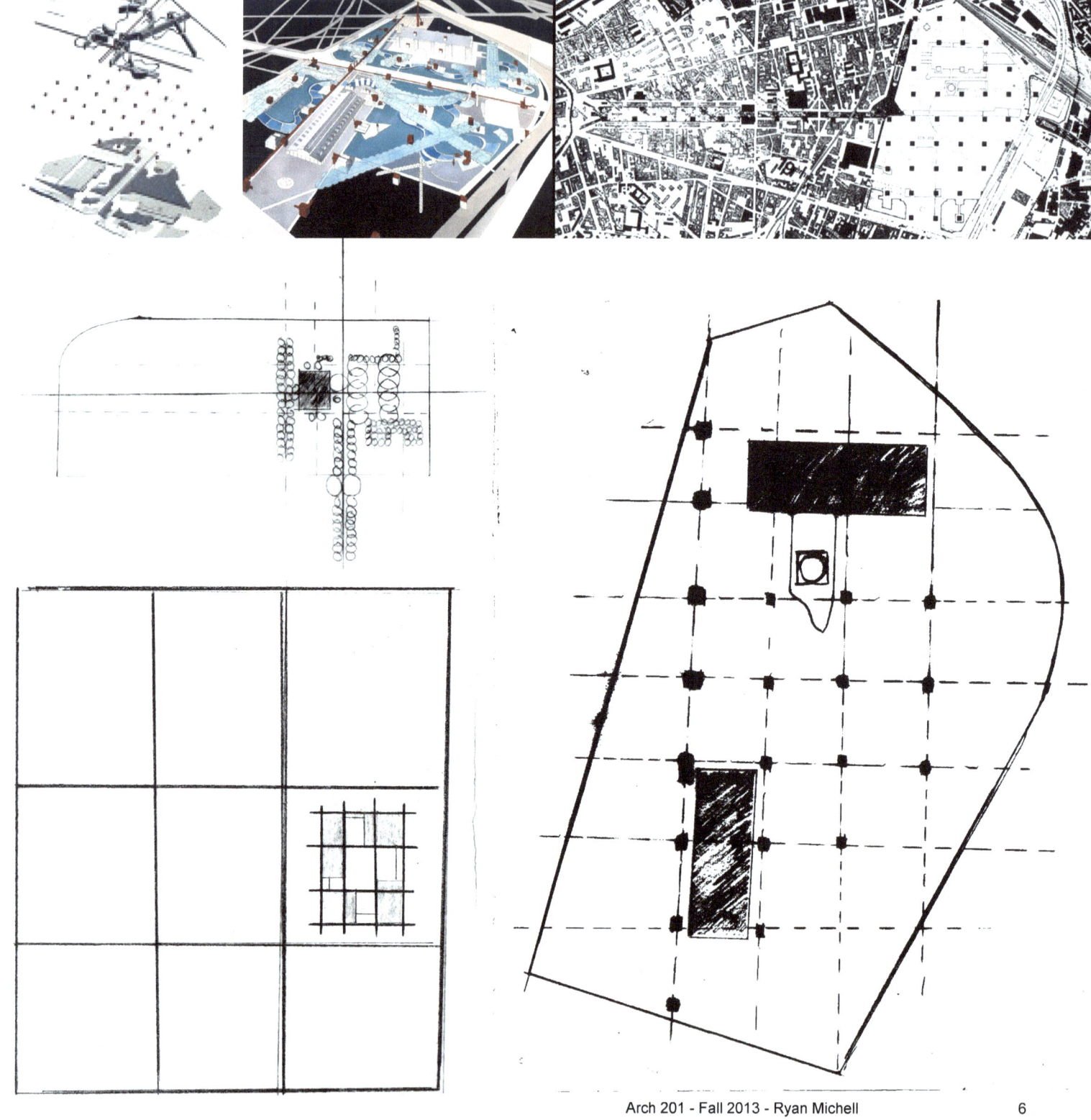

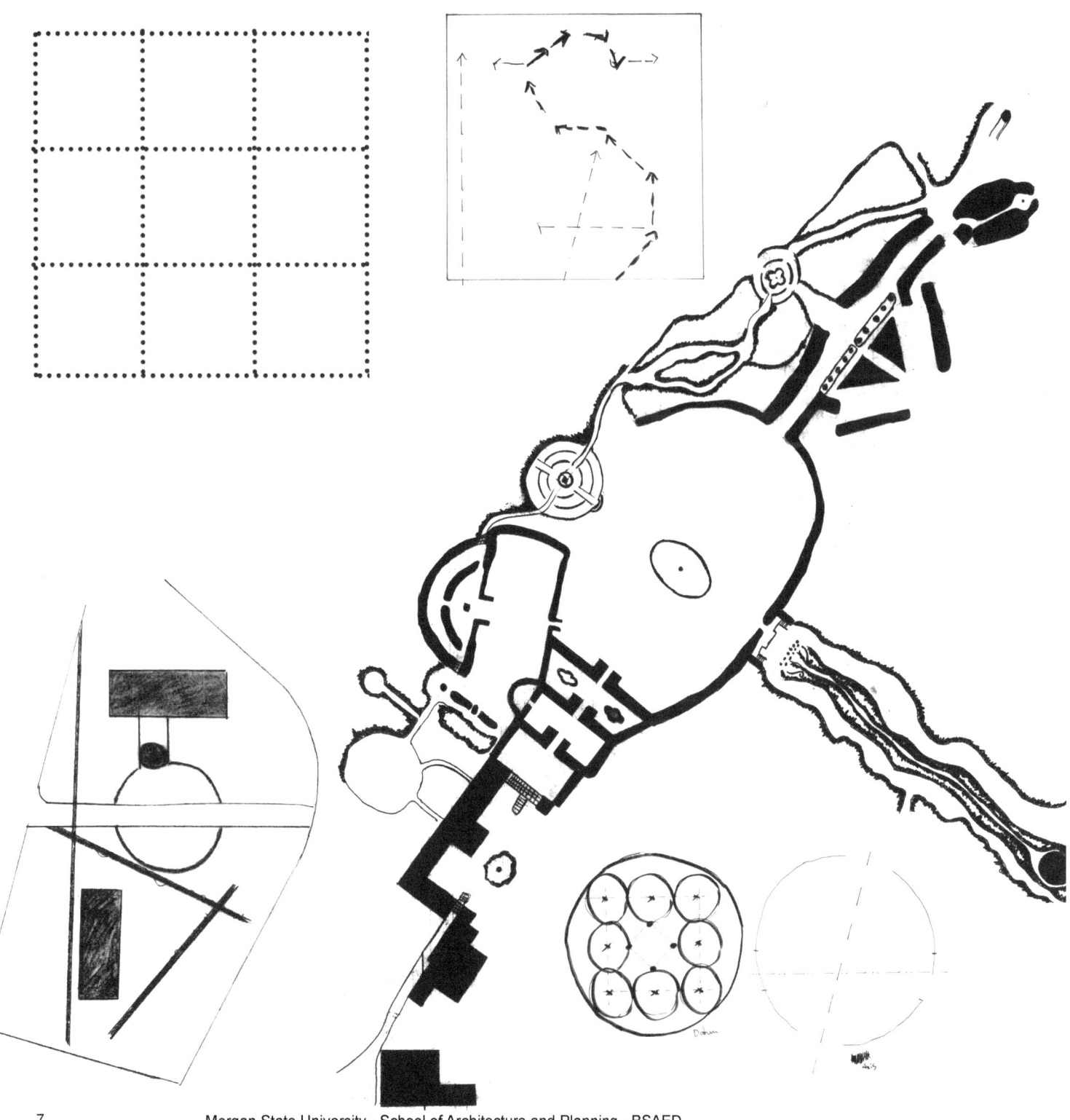

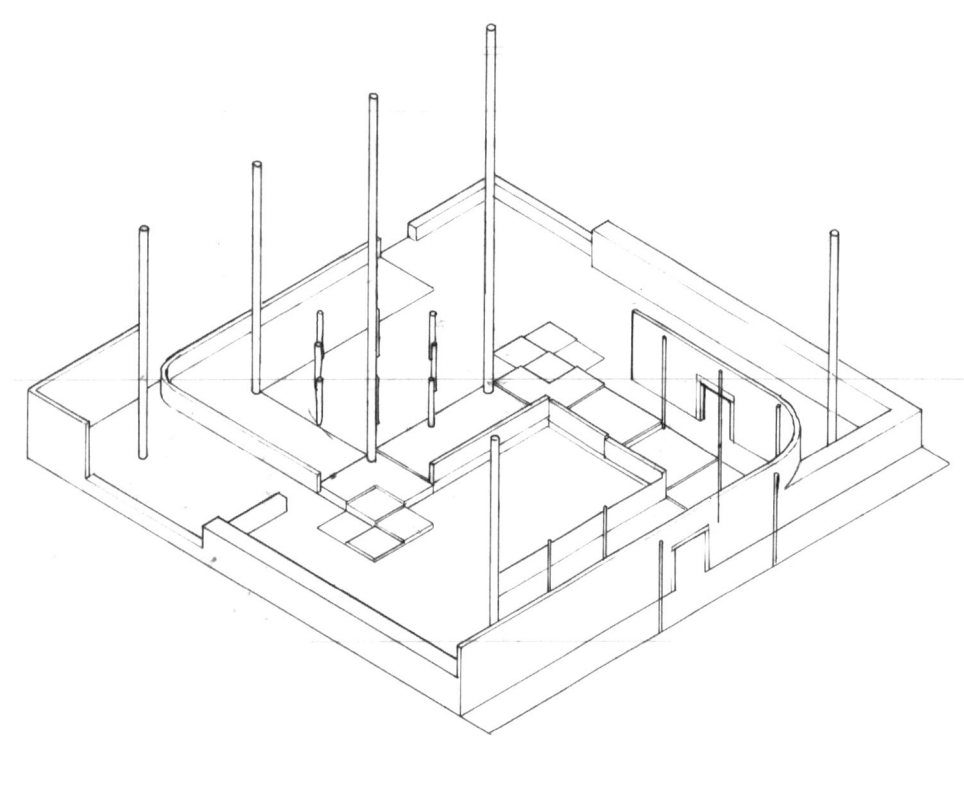

Page Left: Diagramtic anaylsis of Ladew Gardens and ordering diagrams upon which design itterations grew out of.

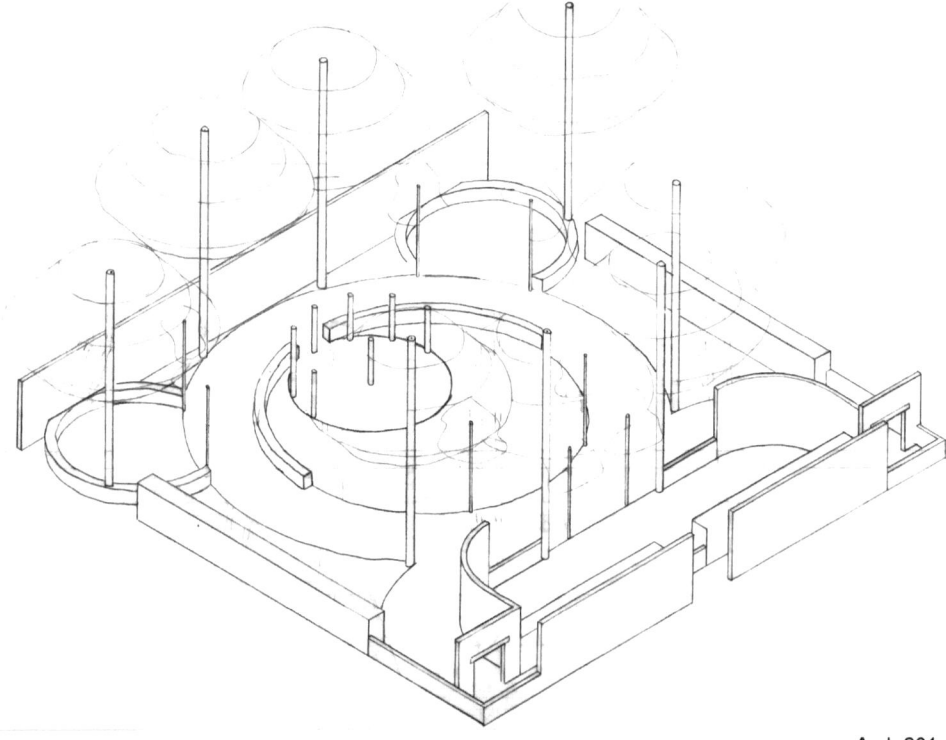

Left: Early option axonometric explorations. Each attempt sought to create a meandering/contemplative circulation and isolated secondary space that strictly conformed to a regulating grid.

A series of perspective drawings showing wayfinding elements such as wall/window openings and seating that help form the secondary spaces.

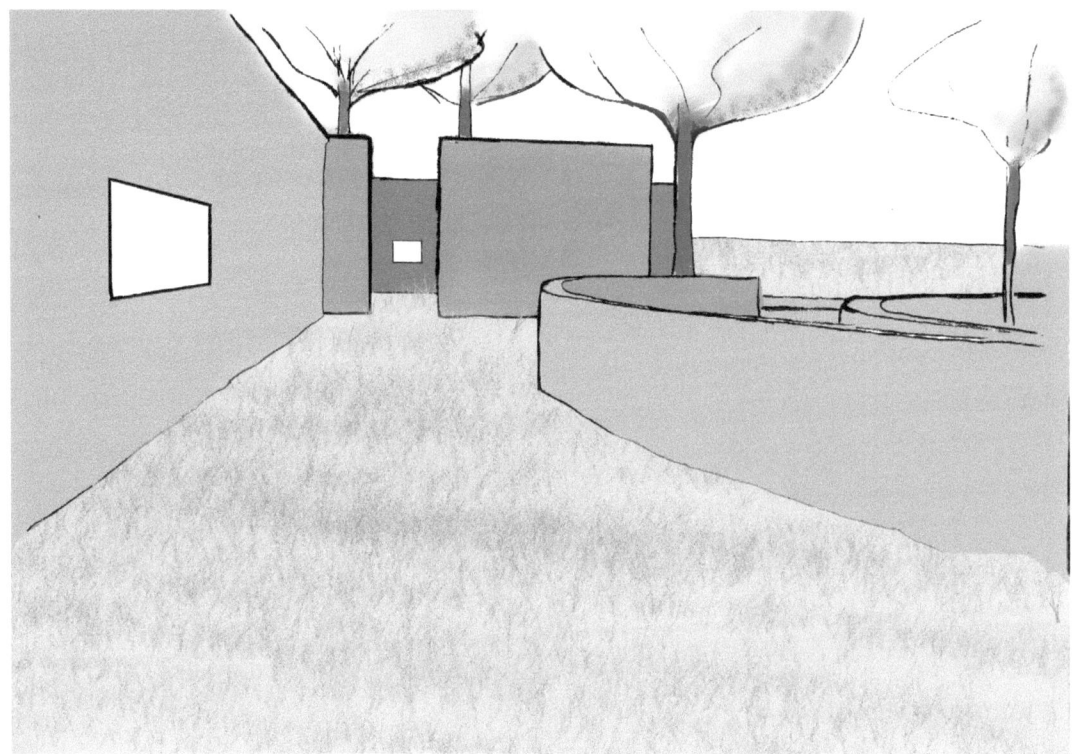

A depiction of the terminus of the main path through the space ending at a circular reflecting pool.

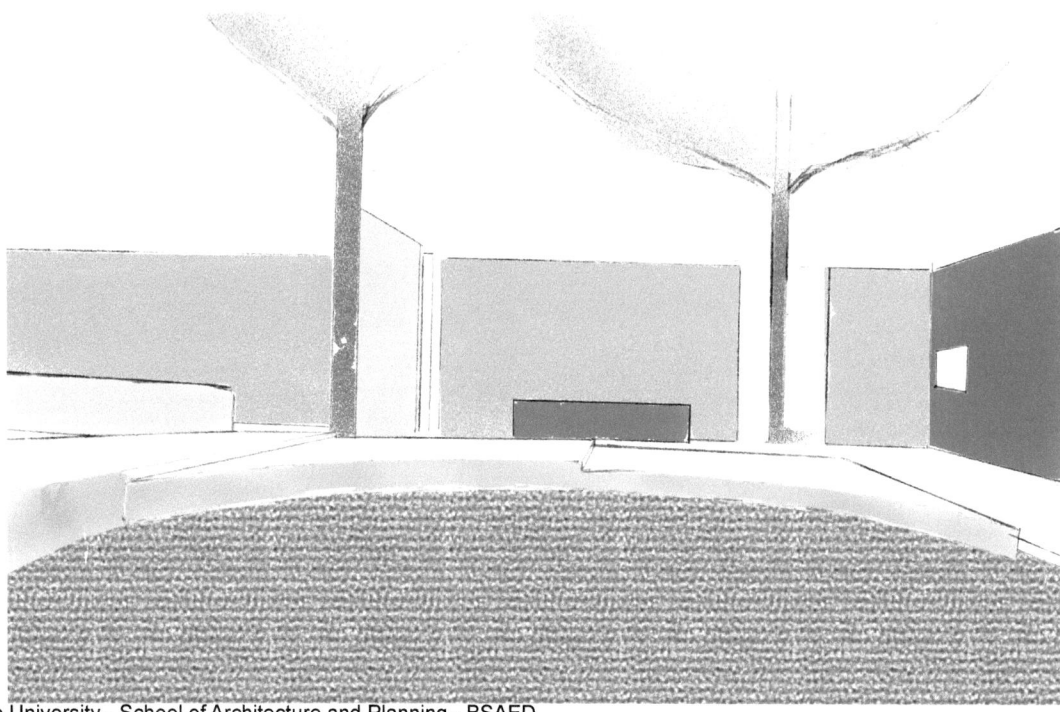

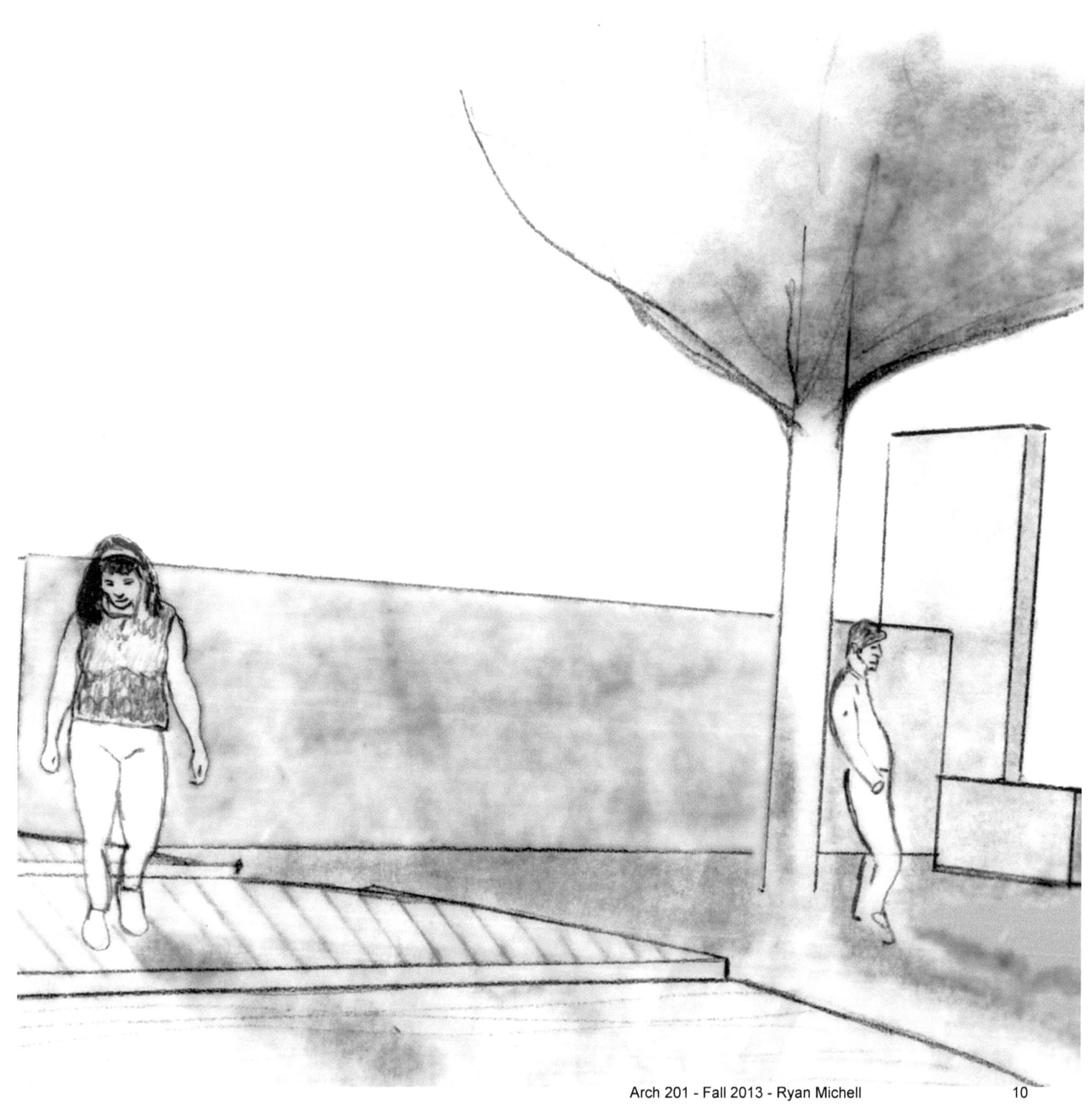

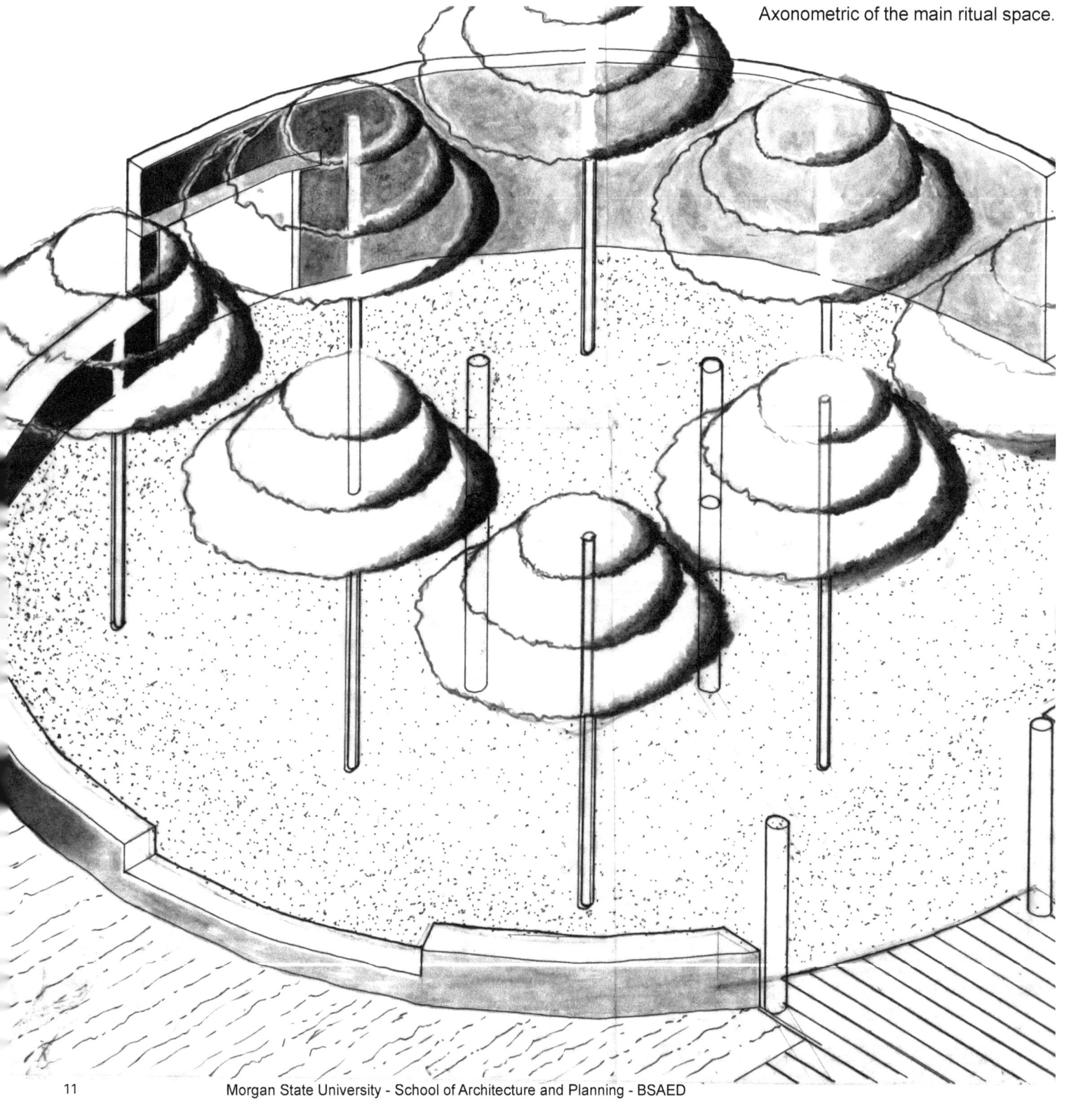

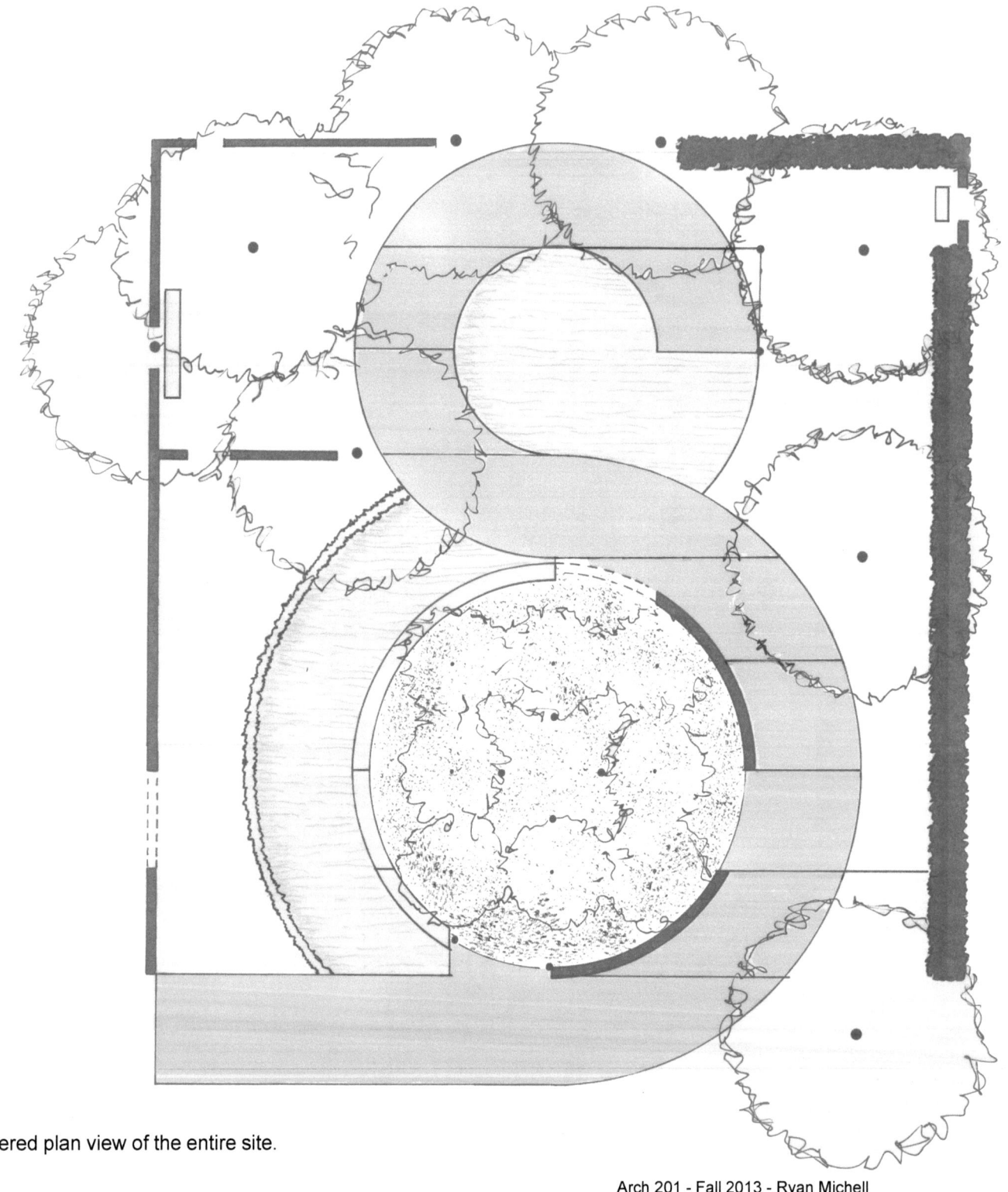

Rendered plan view of the entire site.

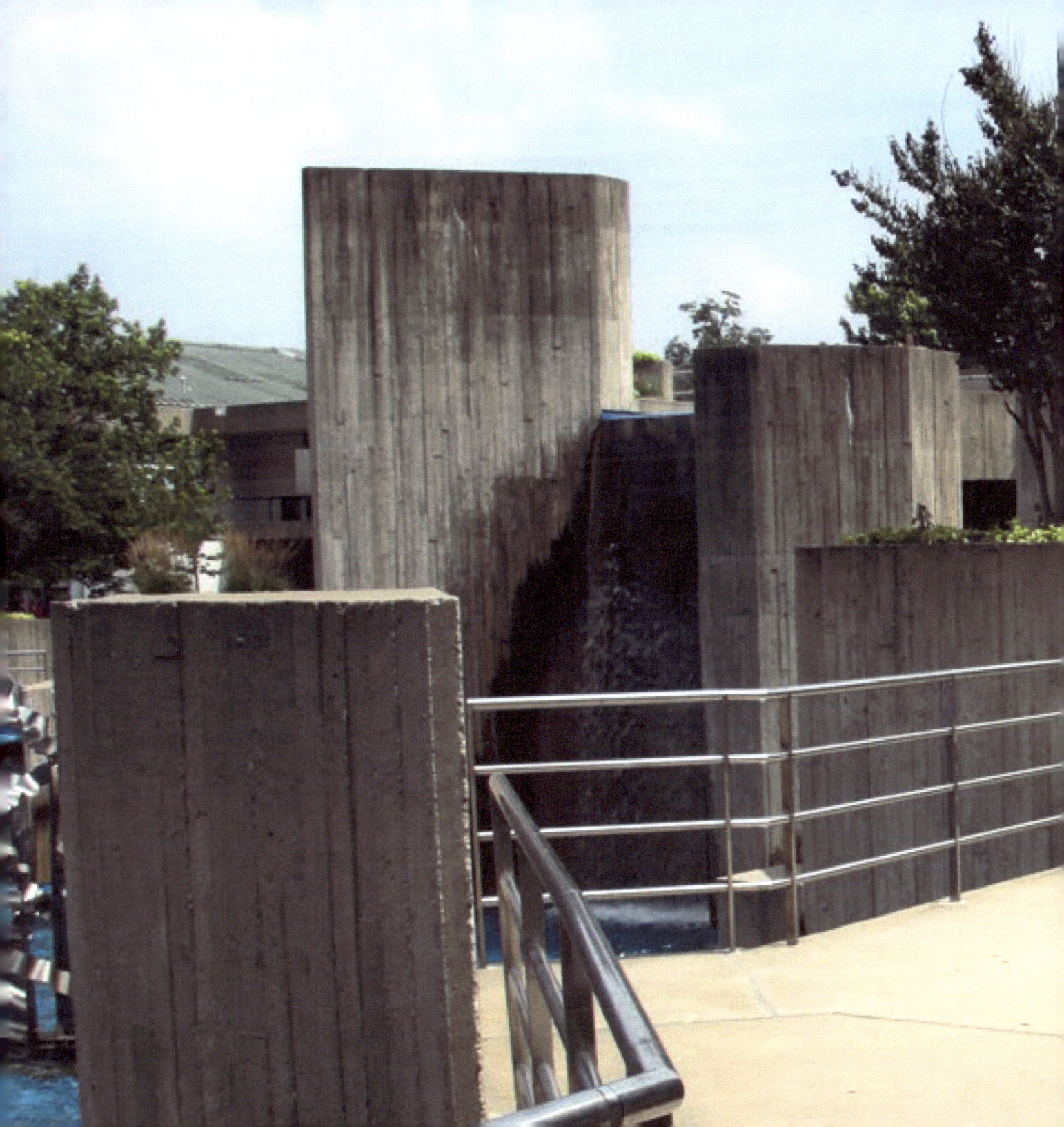

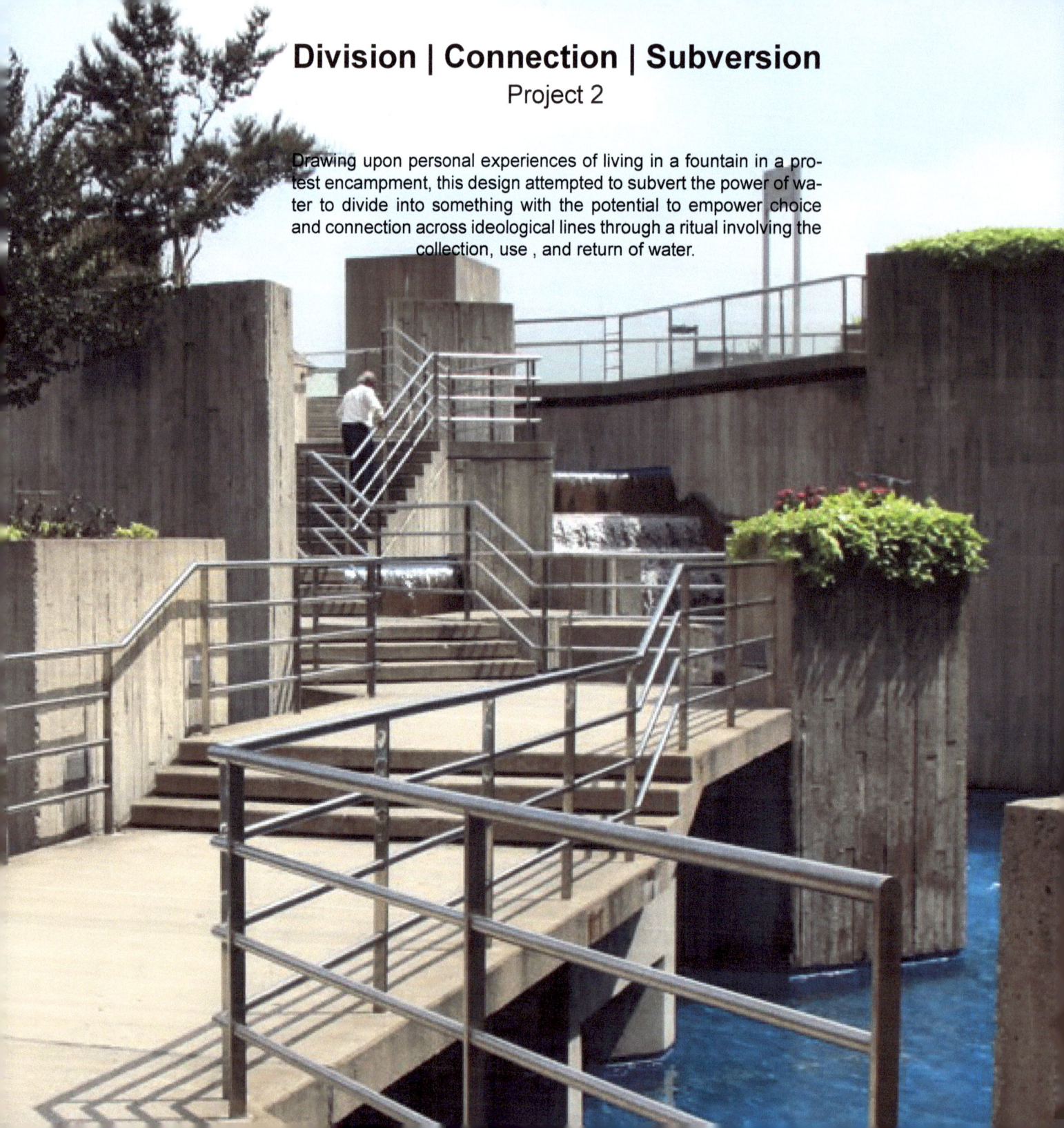

Division | Connection | Subversion
Project 2

Drawing upon personal experiences of living in a fountain in a protest encampment, this design attempted to subvert the power of water to divide into something with the potential to empower choice and connection across ideological lines through a ritual involving the collection, use , and return of water.

Early options attempting to join or negotiate space bifurcated by water.

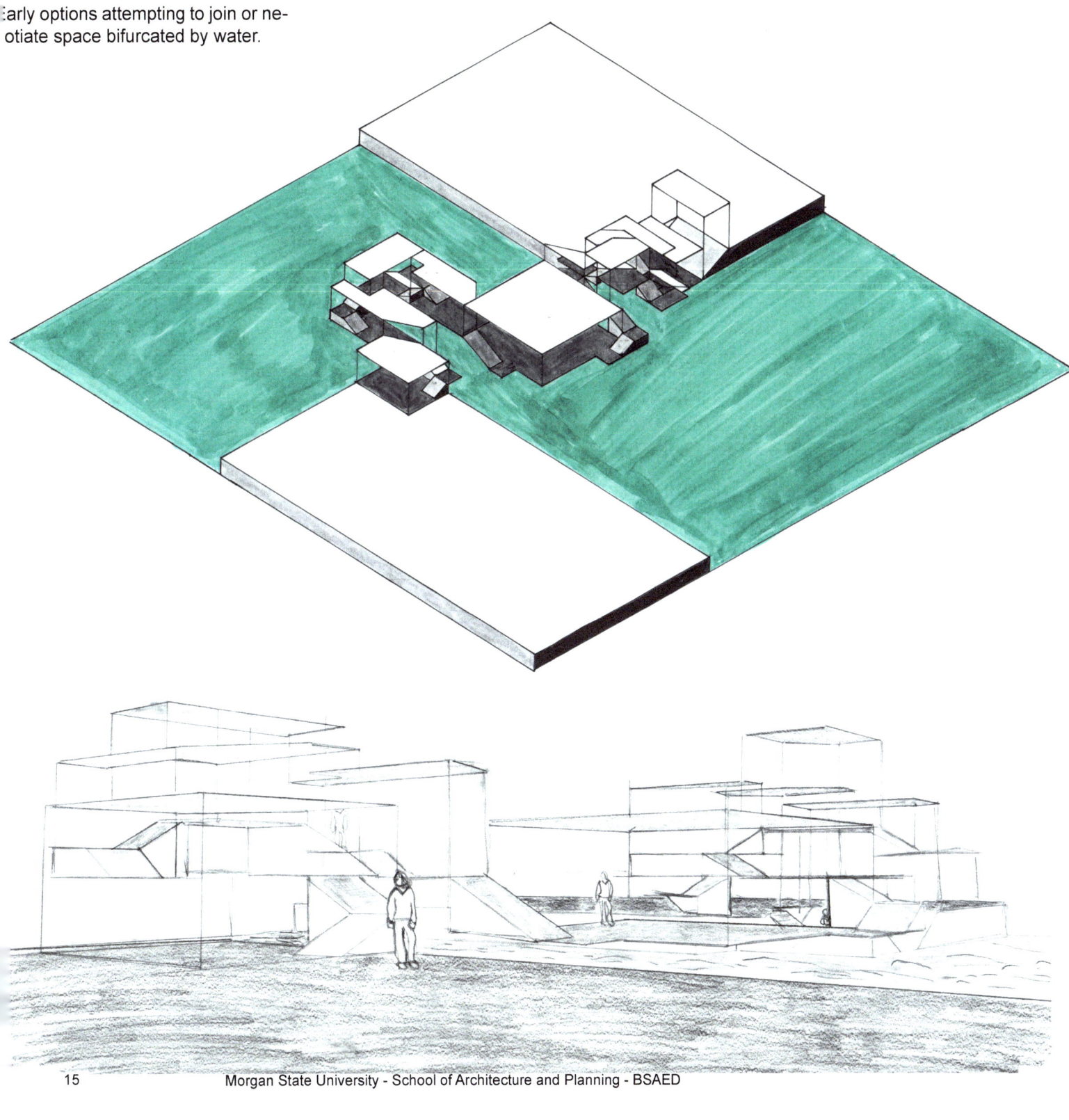

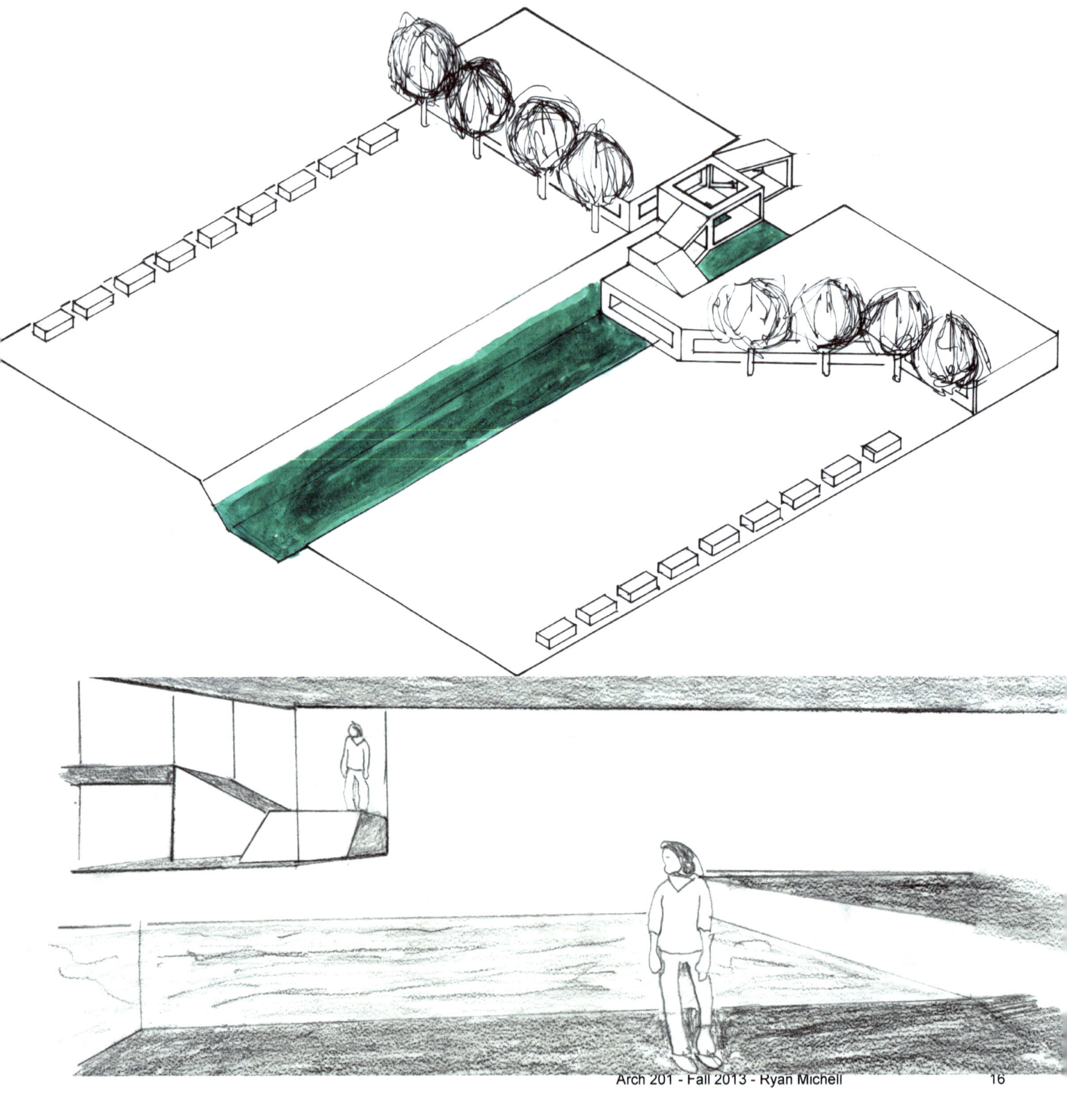

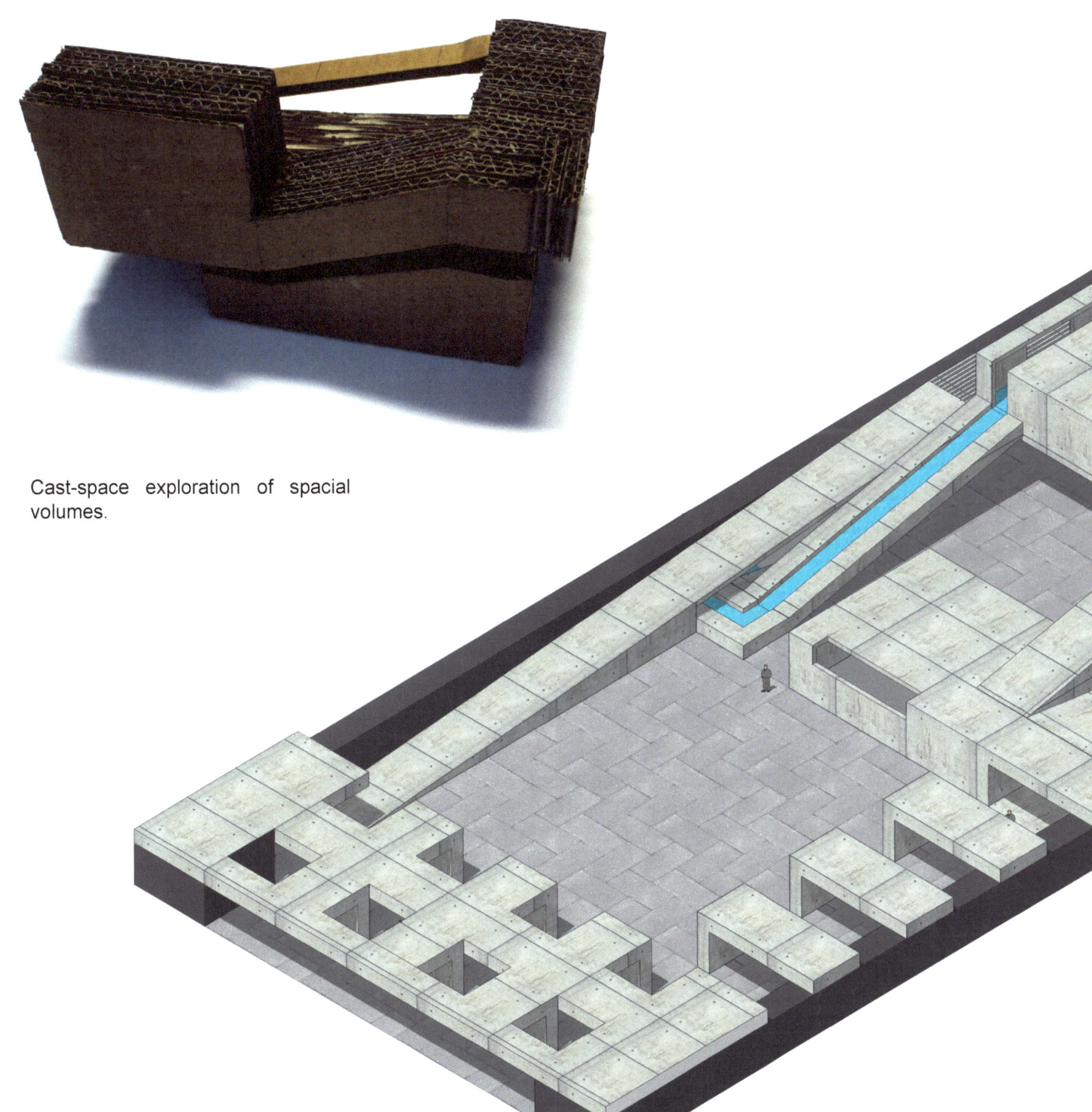

Cast-space exploration of spacial volumes.

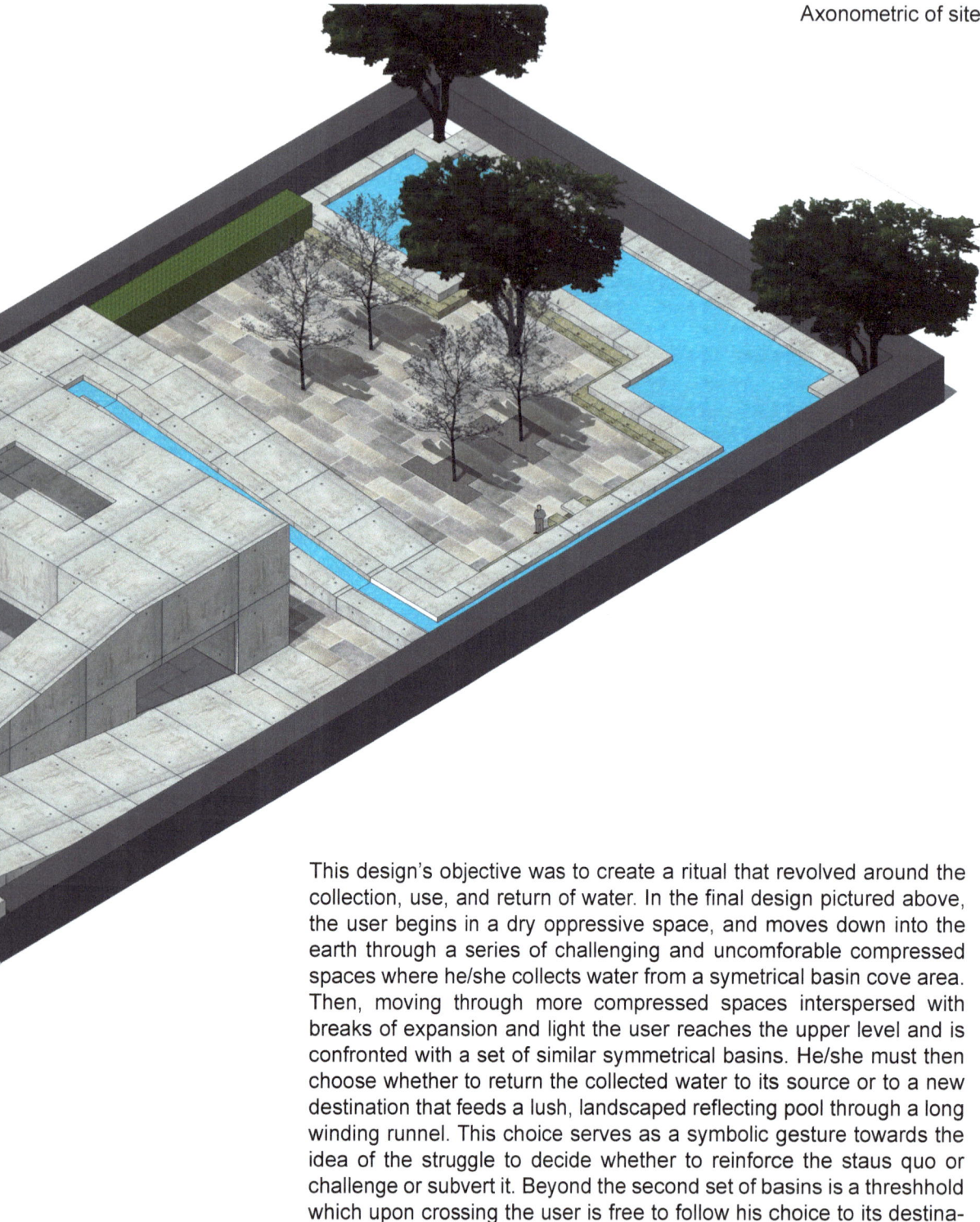

This design's objective was to create a ritual that revolved around the collection, use, and return of water. In the final design pictured above, the user begins in a dry oppressive space, and moves down into the earth through a series of challenging and uncomfortable compressed spaces where he/she collects water from a symetrical basin cove area. Then, moving through more compressed spaces interspersed with breaks of expansion and light the user reaches the upper level and is confronted with a set of similar symmetrical basins. He/she must then choose whether to return the collected water to its source or to a new destination that feeds a lush, landscaped reflecting pool through a long winding runnel. This choice serves as a symbolic gesture towards the idea of the struggle to decide whether to reinforce the staus quo or challenge or subvert it. Beyond the second set of basins is a threshhold which upon crossing the user is free to follow his choice to its destination.

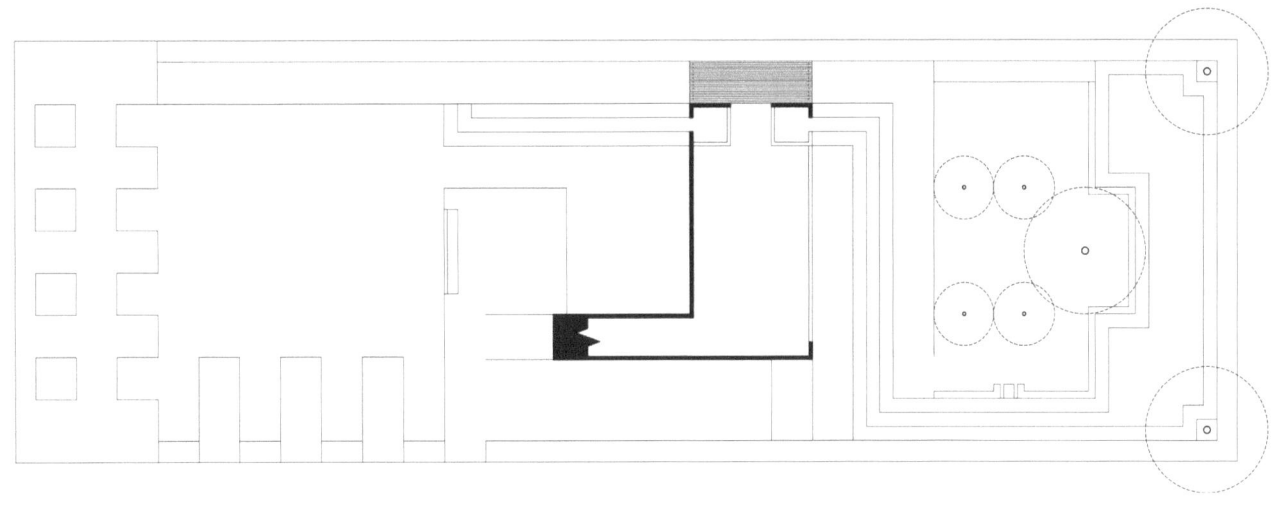

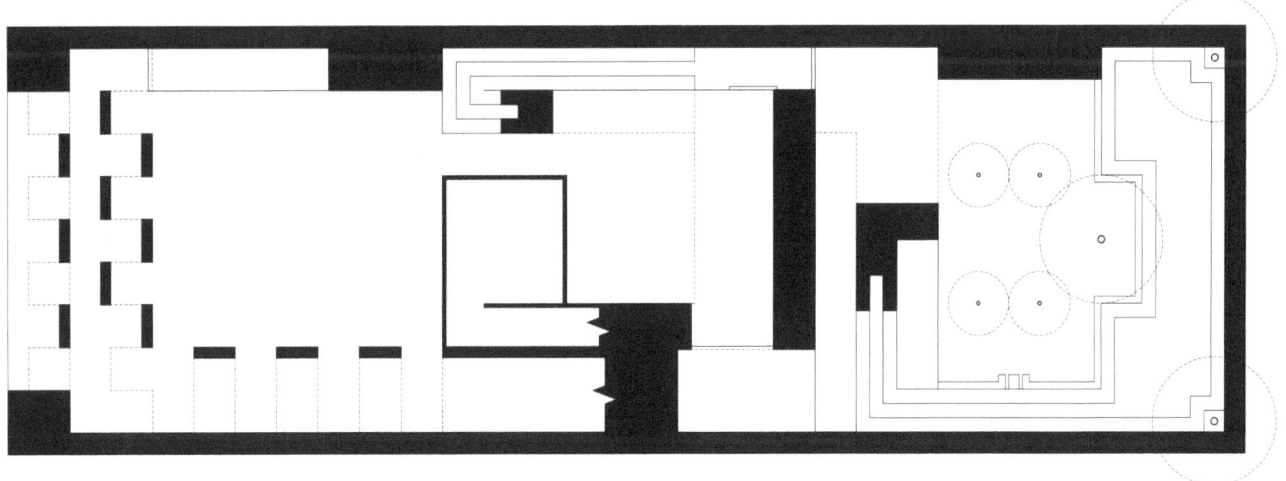

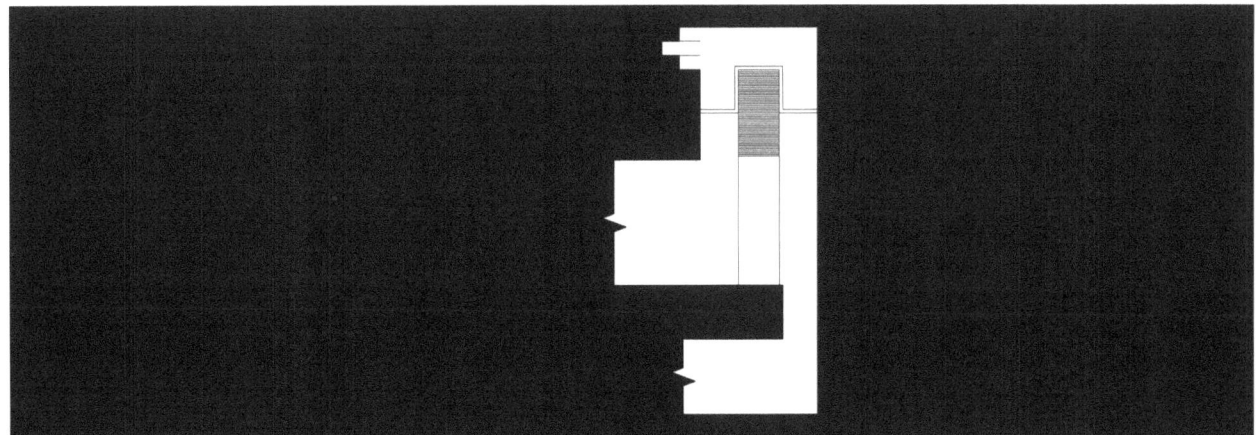

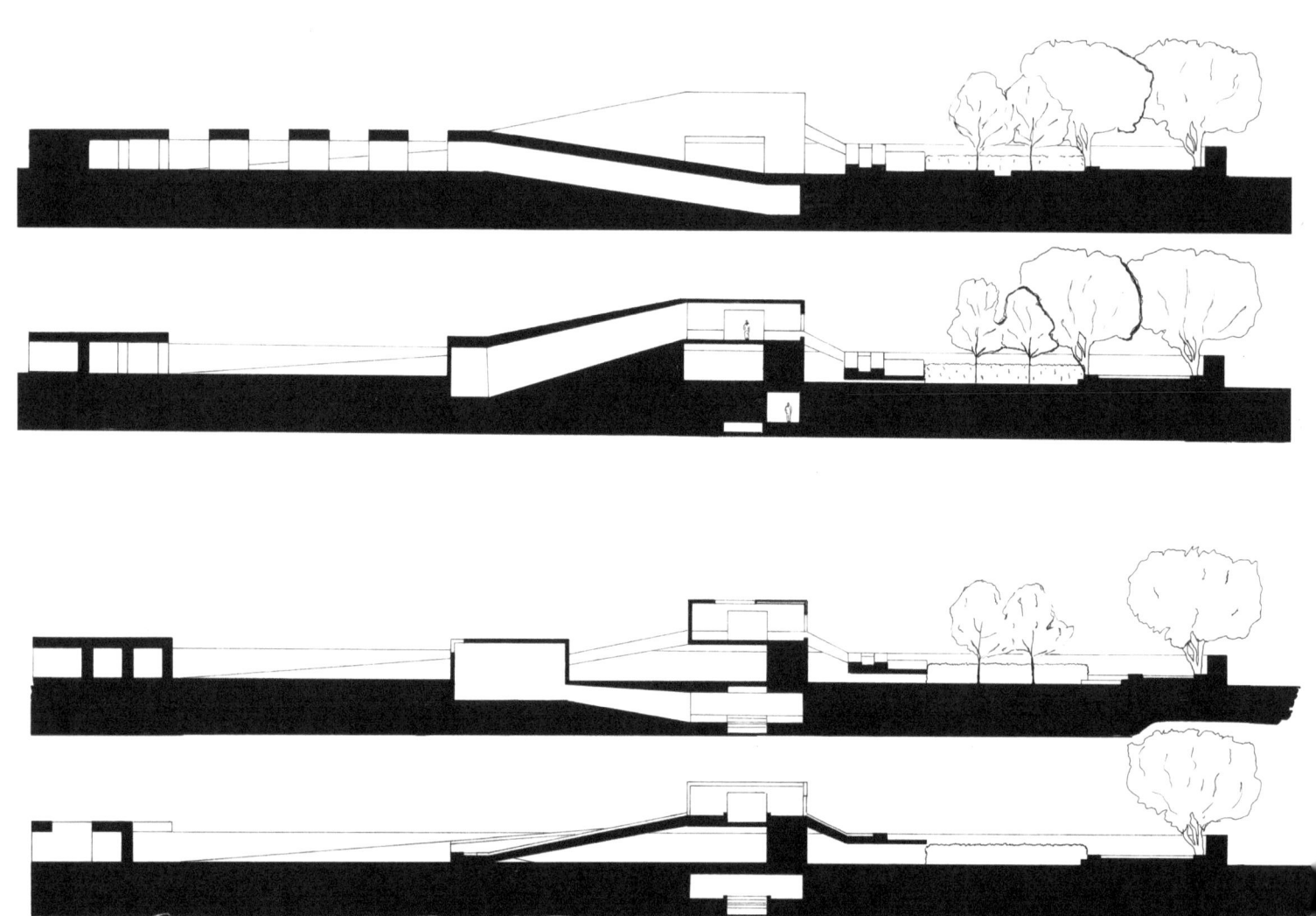

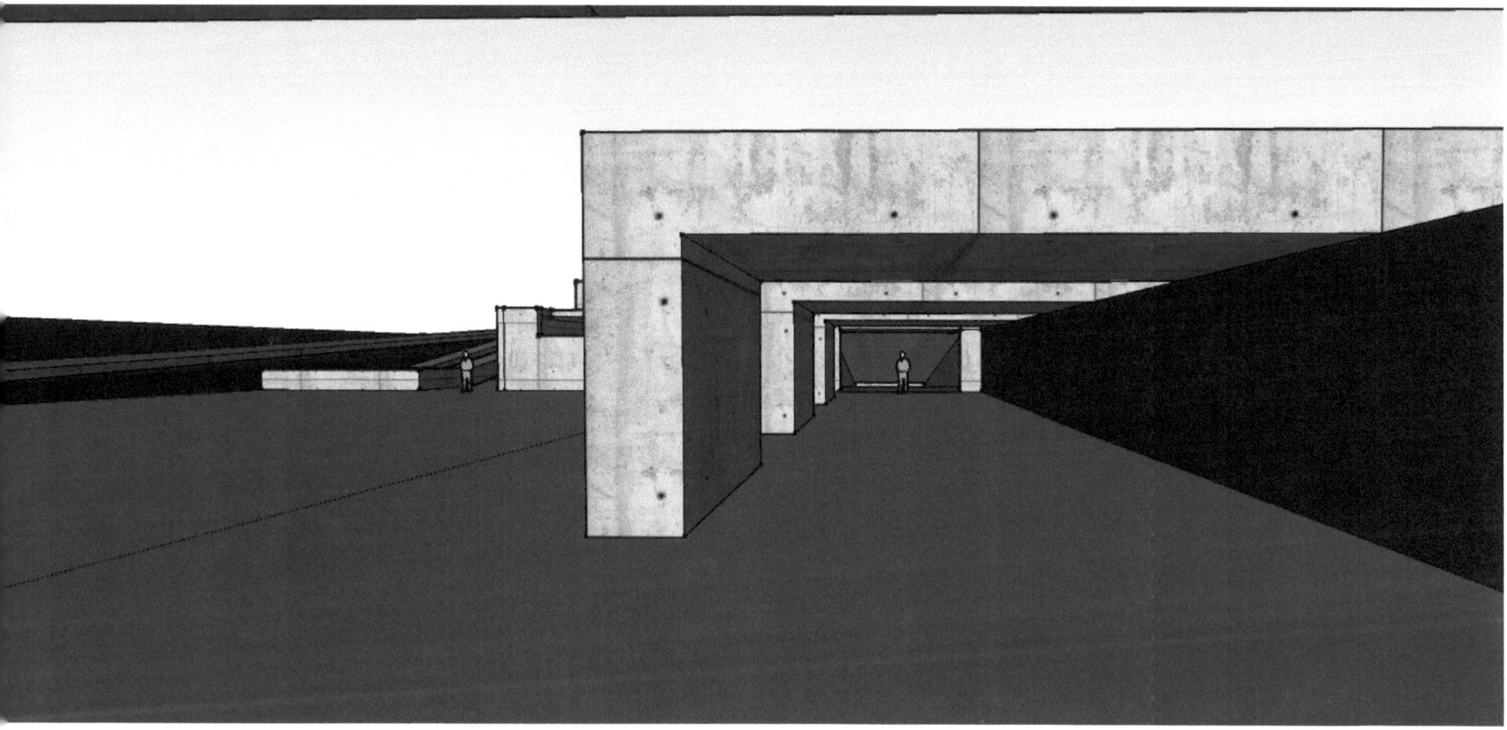

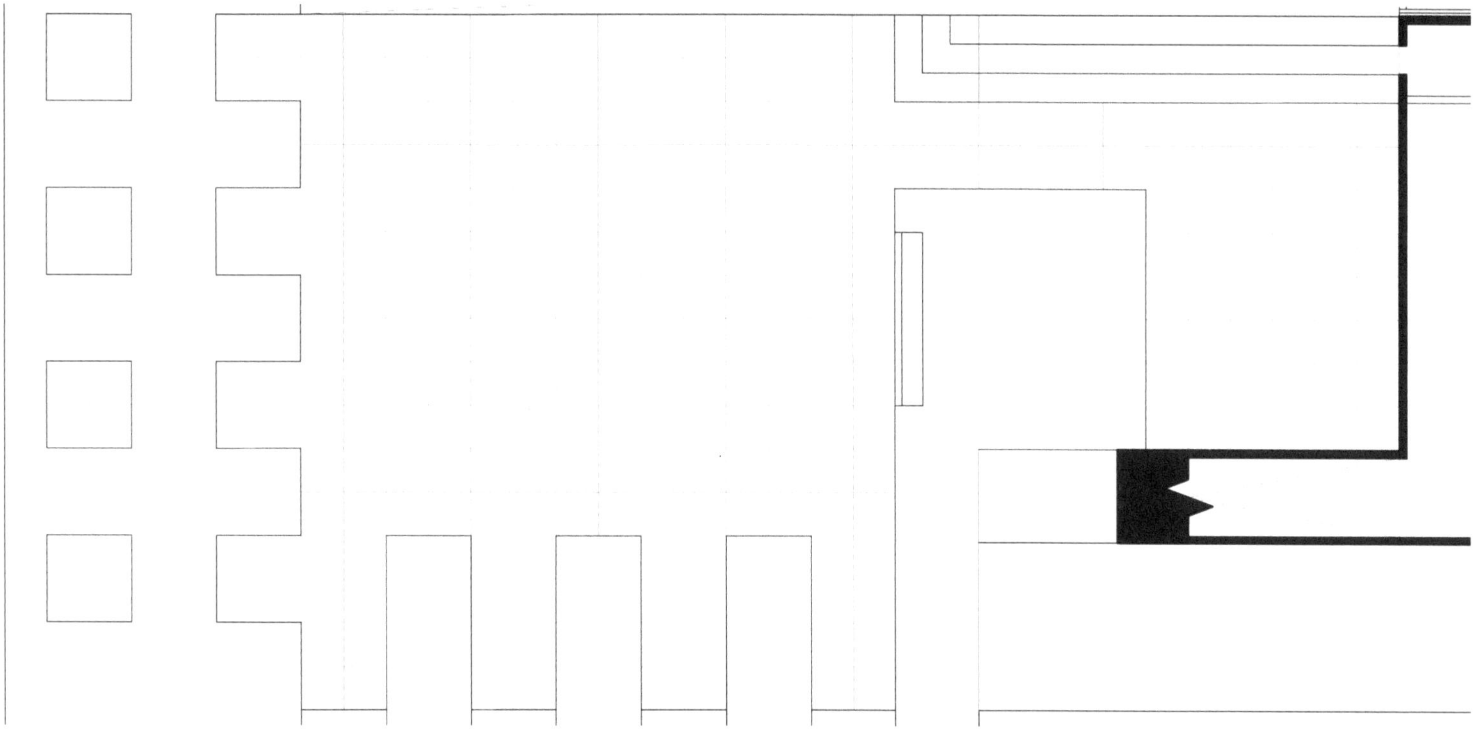

Morgan State University - School of Architecture and Planning - BSAED

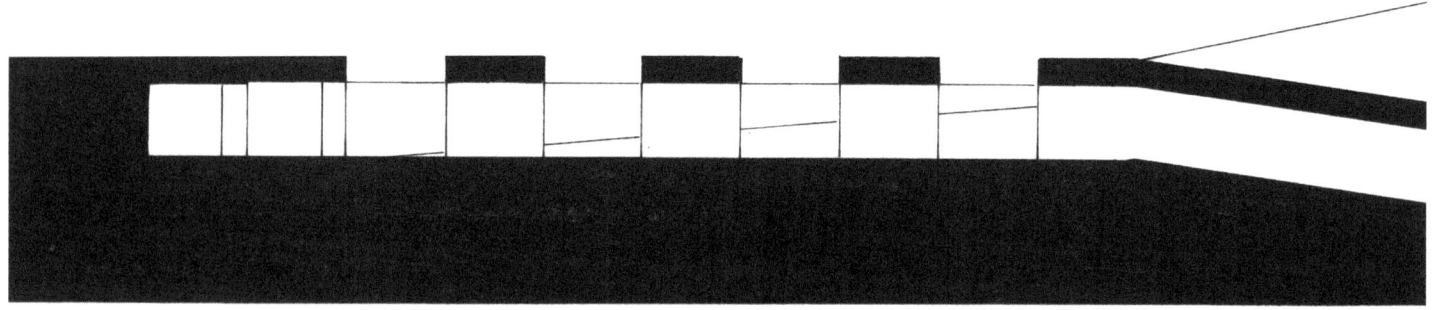

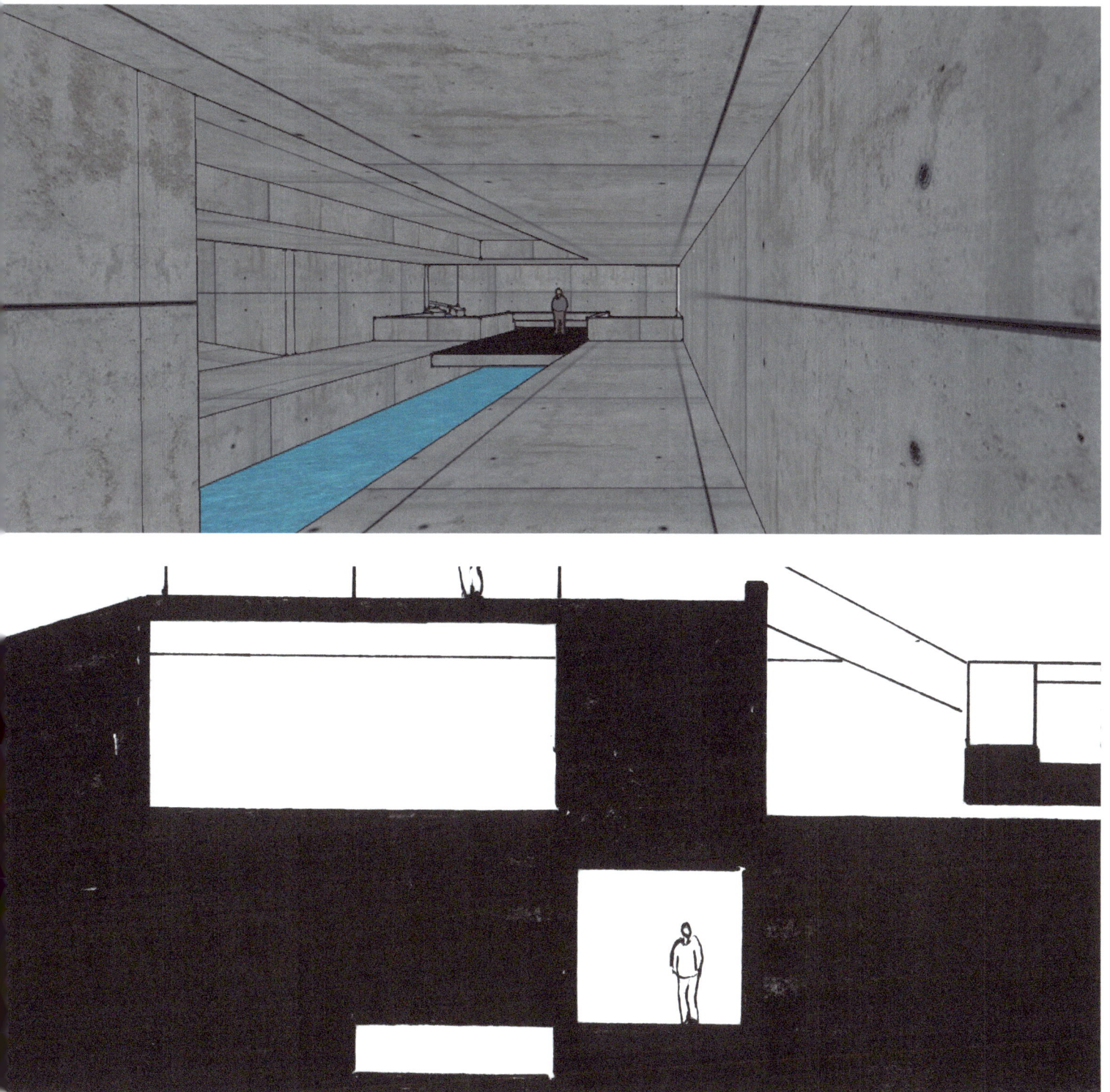

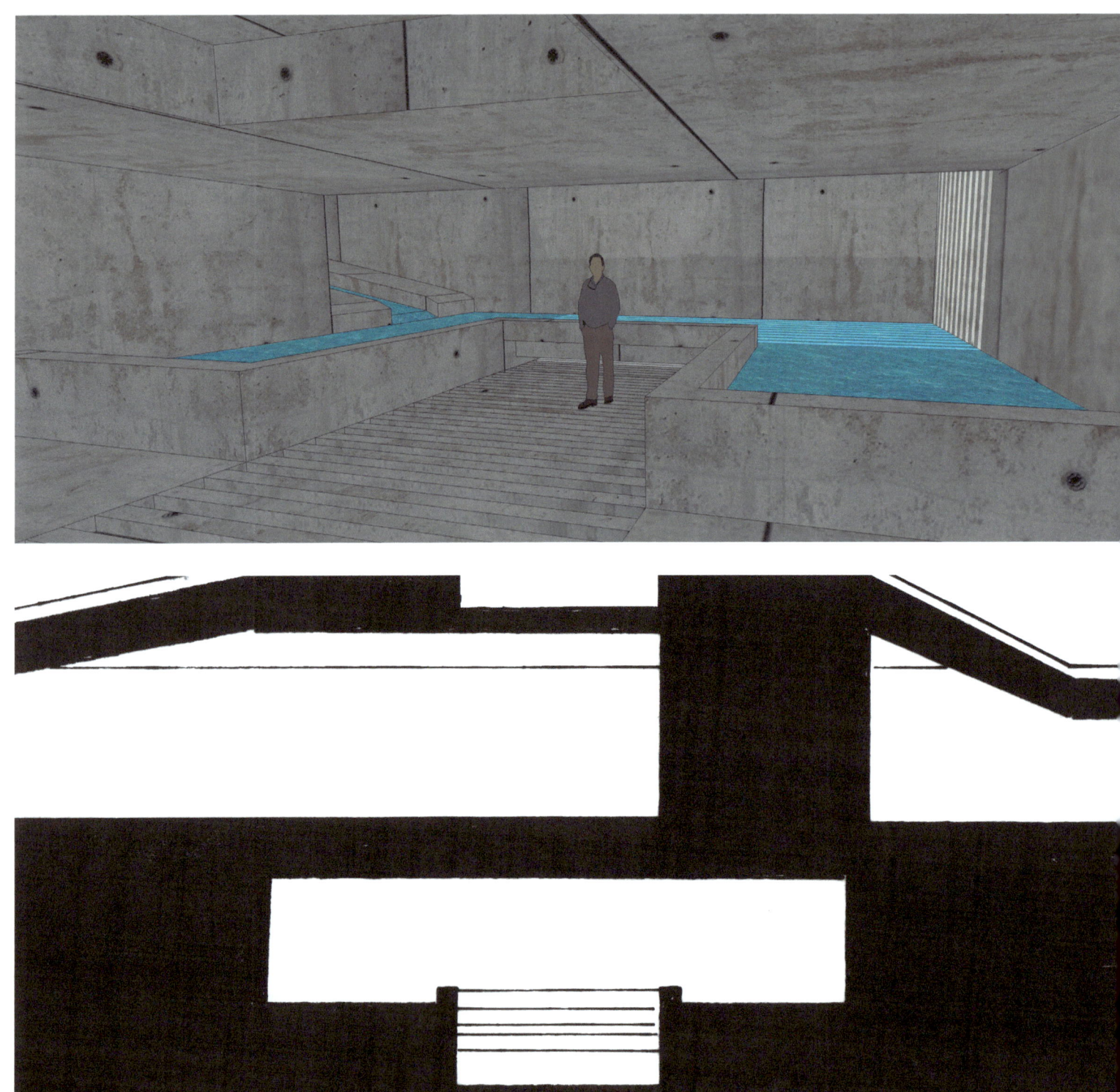

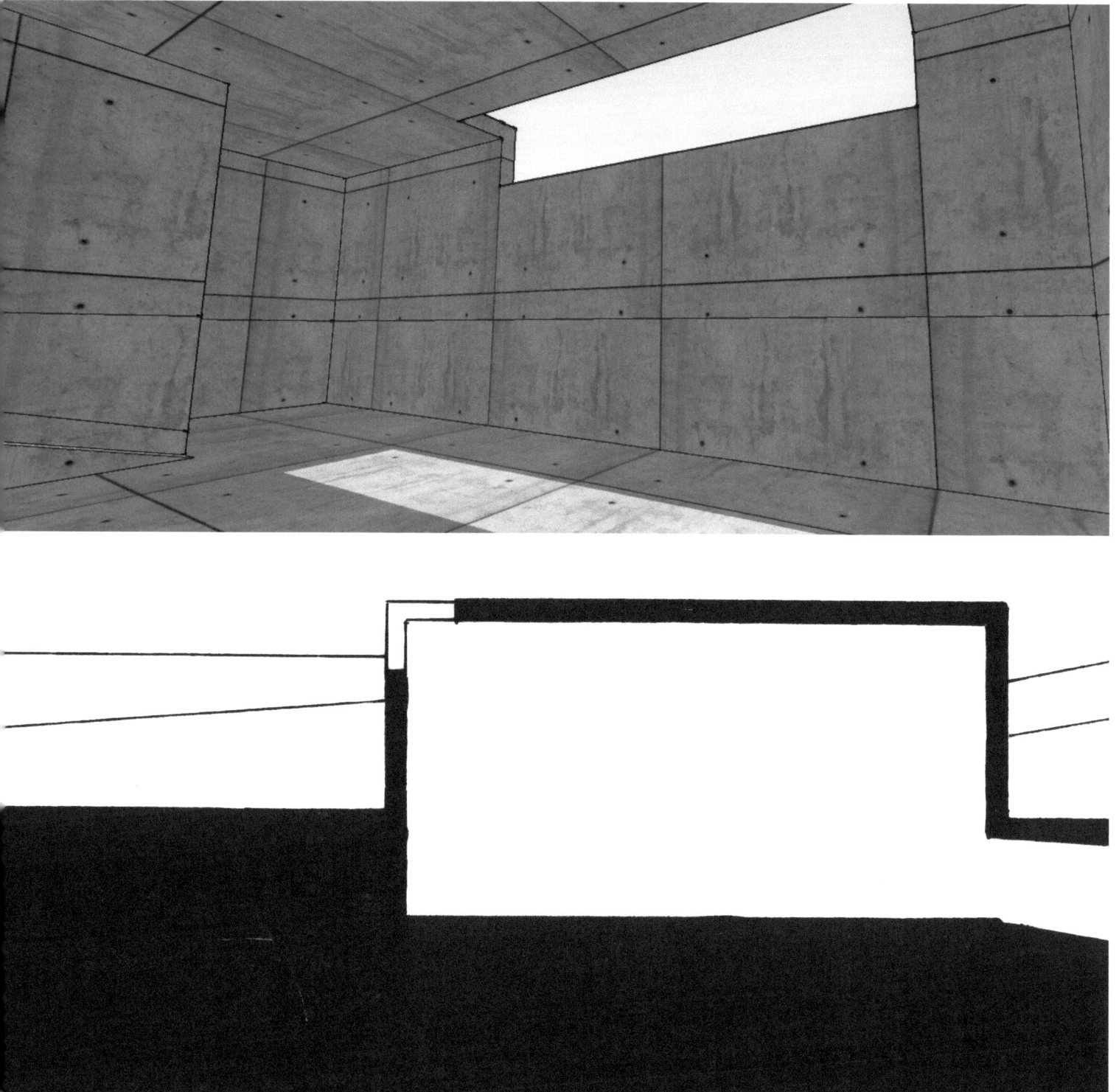

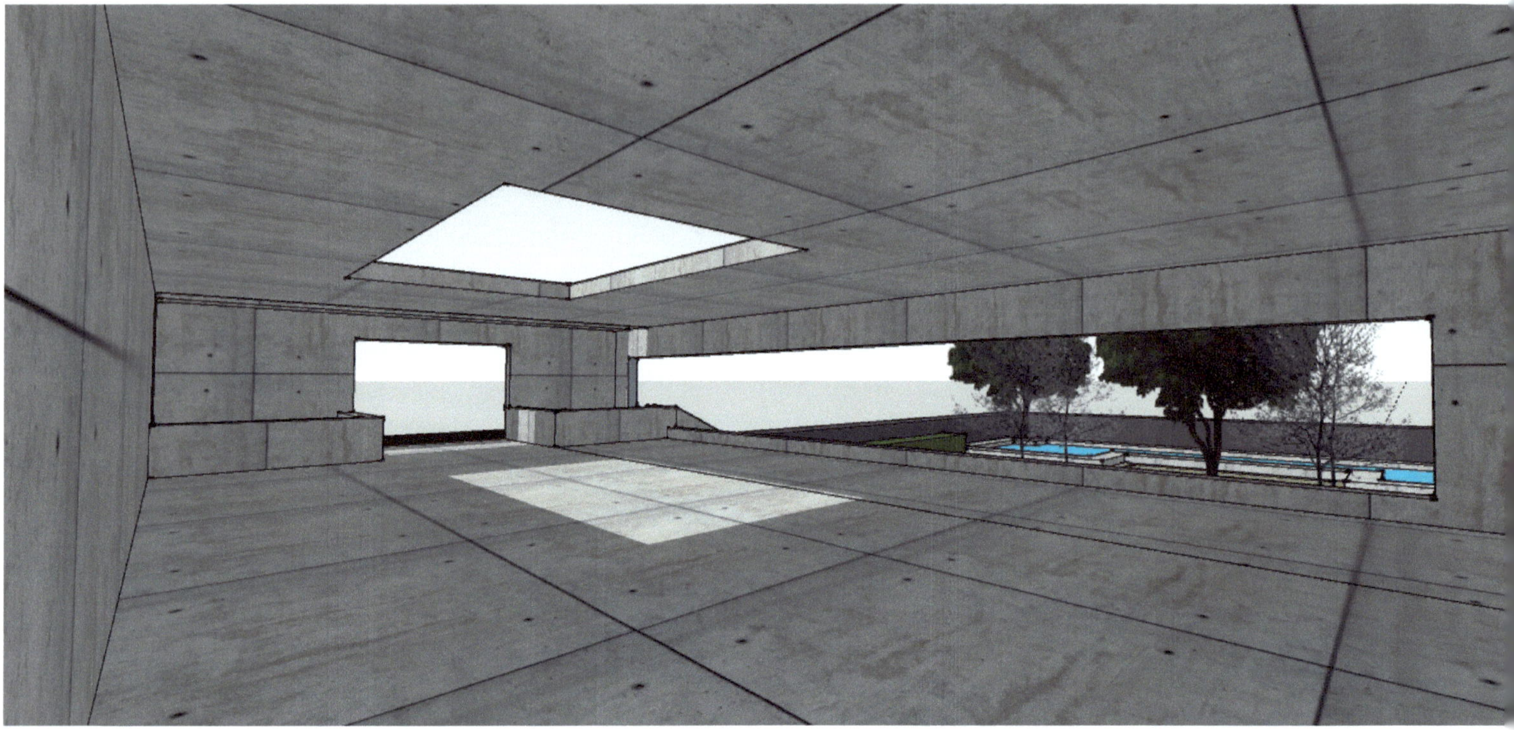

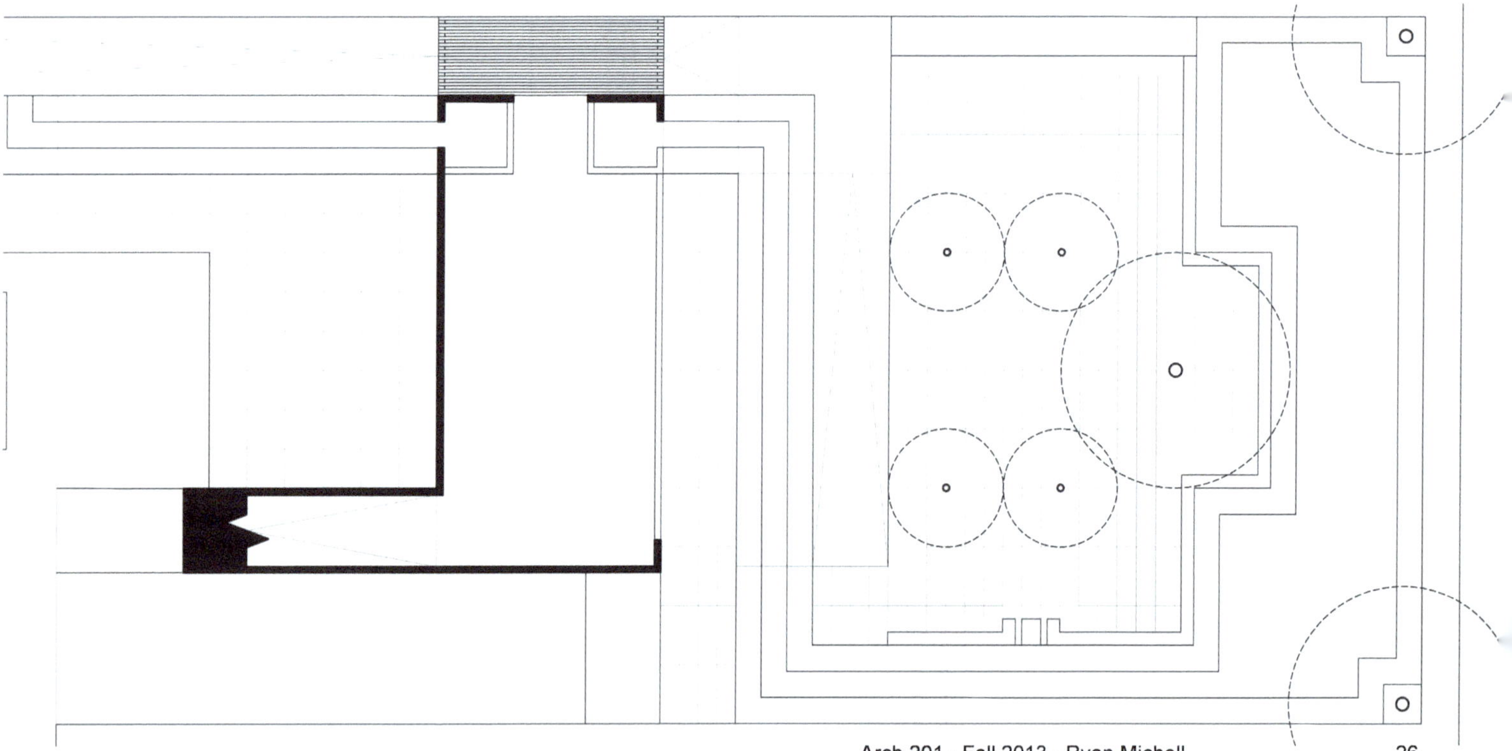

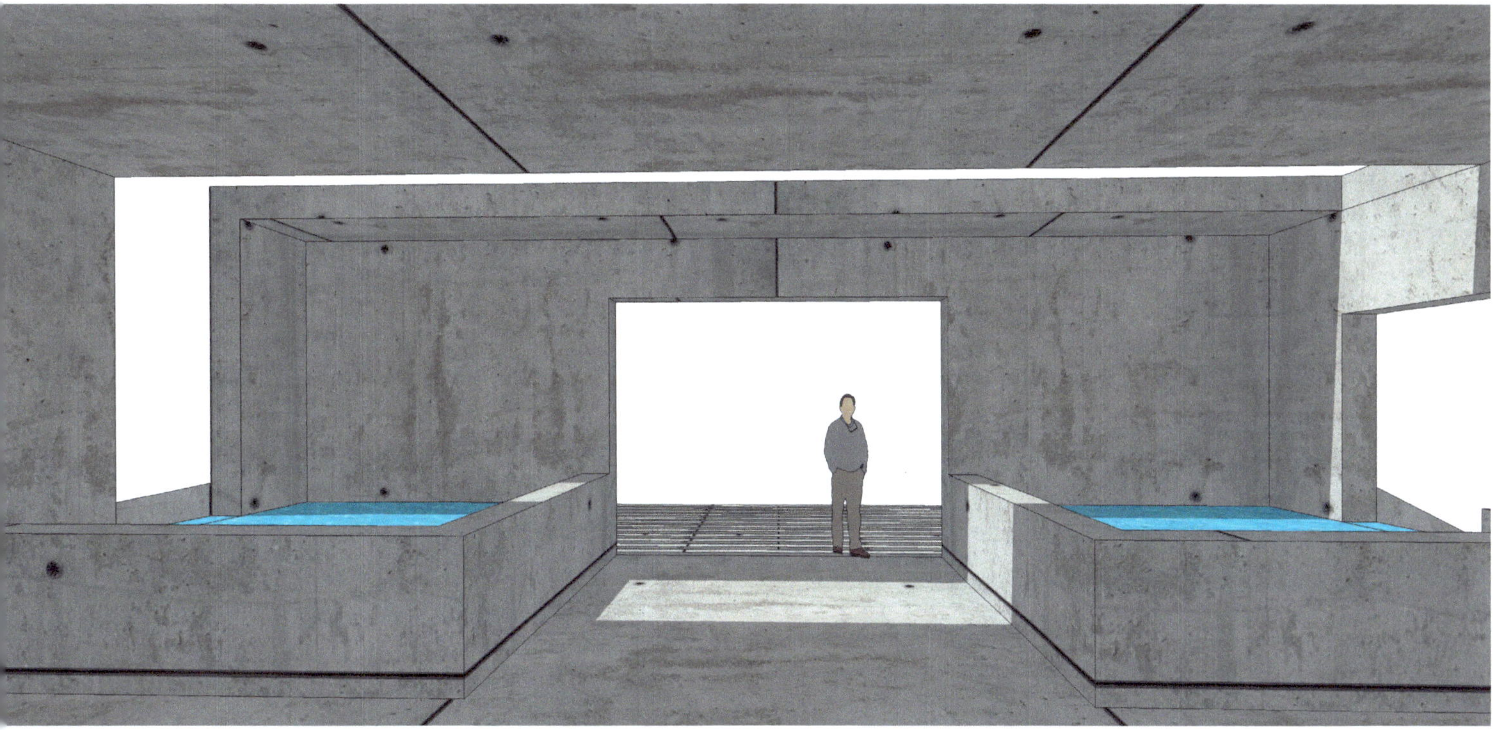

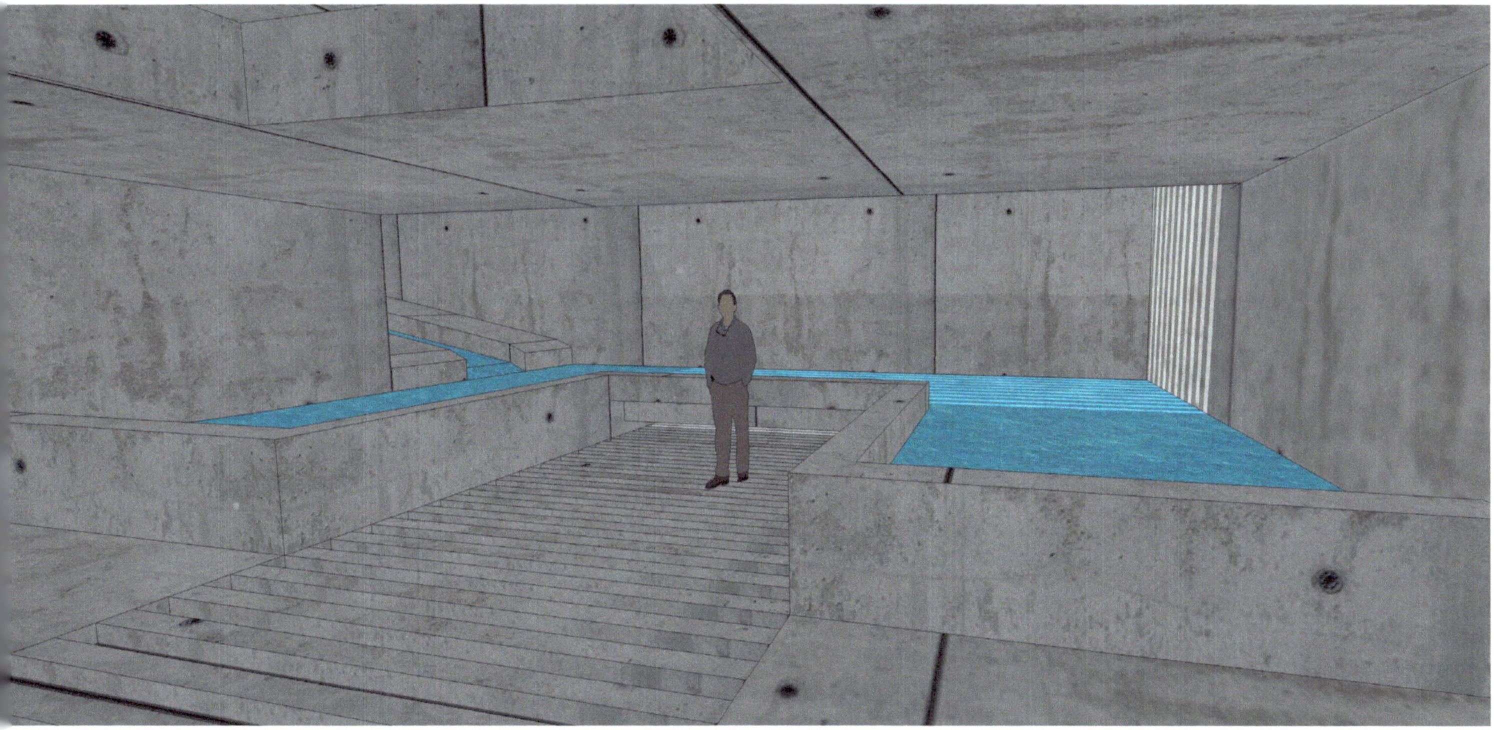

Morgan State University - School of Architecture and Planning - BSAED

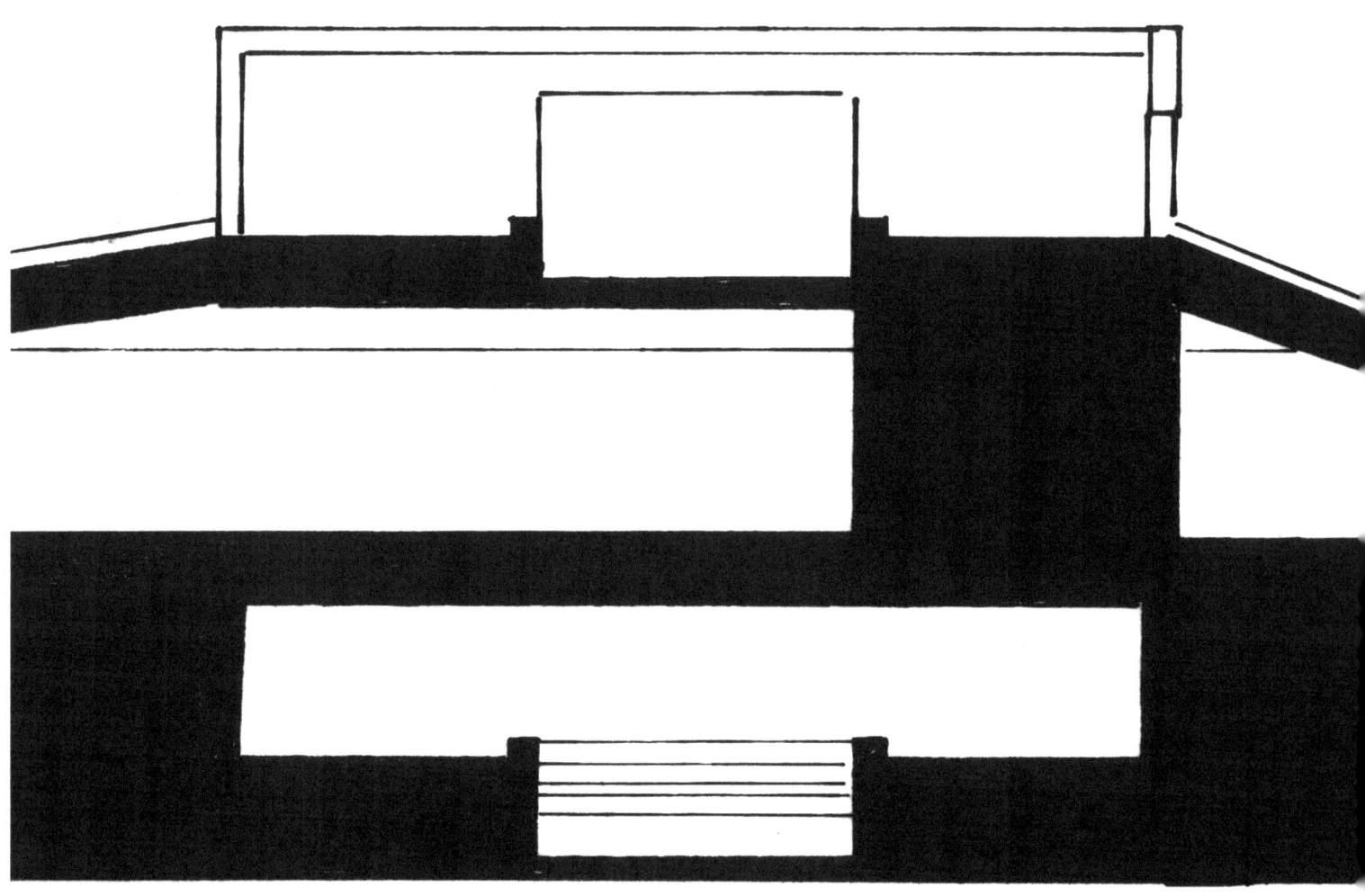

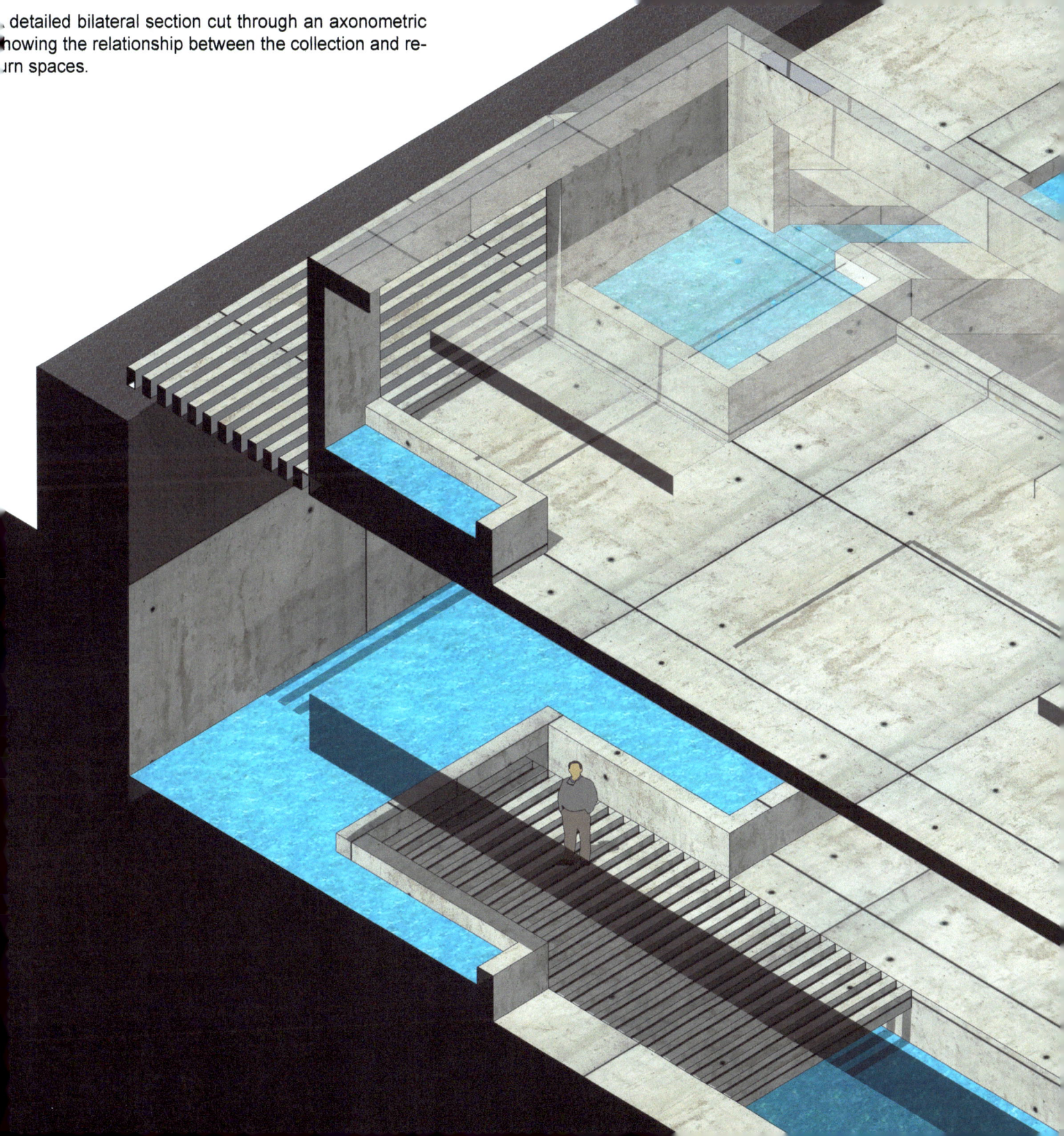

A detailed bilateral section cut through an axonometric showing the relationship between the collection and re- turn spaces.

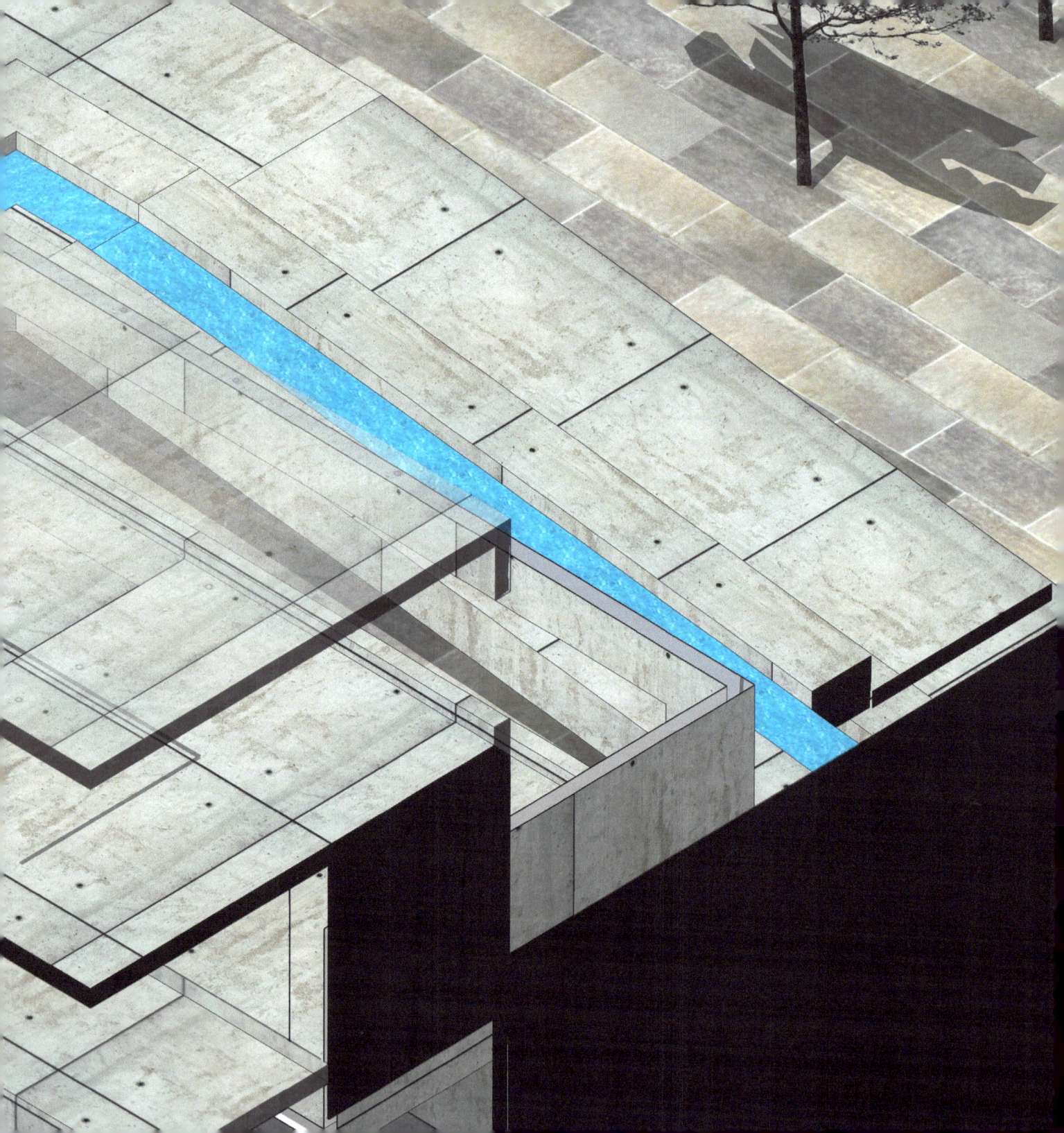

www.ingramcontent.com/pod-product-compliance
Lightning Source LLC
Chambersburg PA
CBHW041301180526
45172CB00003B/926